Born On A Mountaintop

David Owen Ferrier

Marti,

I thank you
for your support

Battle Press
SATELLITE BEACH, FLORIDA

Read On

Born On A Mountaintop

Battle Press books may be ordered through booksellers or by contacting:

Battle Press
1588 Highway A1A #B
Satellite Beach, FL 32937
1-919-218-4039
www.battlepress.media

ISBN: 978-1-5136-6802-4 (softcover).

Library of Congress Control Number: 2020918550.

First Edition

Cover Photo:

The Author with Claus

Pollards Basement

Lowell, Mass

Chrissmassy 1951

Santa Wears a Timex?

Sing in me Muse, of Days of Yore,

When lies were told to Children,

To keep them from becoming Wise

Dedicated To:

The Children Who Lived Through It All

The Times They Were A-Changing

TABLE OF CONTENTS

ACKNOWLEDGEMENTS

"The fountains of my great deep are broken up and have rained reminiscences for over 4 and 20 hours. The old life has swept before me like a panorama. The Old Days have trouped by in their Old Glory again. The old faces have looked out of the mists of the past. Old footsteps have sounded in my listening ears. Old hands have clasped mine. Old voices have greeted me and the songs I loved long ago have come wailing down the centuries."

The Great and Powerful, Wizard of Words, American Master and Perpetual Mentor,

Samuel Langhorne Clemens, our beloved Mark Twain.

Also to the Doctors of my Soul, Rick Gallavan and Don Avdul, who walked me through another one.

PROLOGUE

"Born On A Mountain Top" is a reminisce, a personal history sweetened by time, recalled with longing, factual, but not accurate. Those events I have chosen to write about essentially happened, though not necessarily in the idealized manner I have recorded them. It is the issues, the perplexing questions and contradictions I encountered growing up which I have attempted to relate most accurately.

Myths, Good and Evil, customs, traditions, facts and fables, along with not so Little White Lies were a minefield I had to traverse through my childhood. Not all of these fictions were harmful but many were, and I still puzzle over their purpose.

My companions on this journey, as portrayed in these stories, are for the most part, amalgams of my childhood companions. I have chosen to respect their privacy and not inflict my uncertainties and issues onto their journey of growth.

Lowell, Massachusetts remains constant in my memory, a field of clover with considerable puddles of mud and patches of hemlock around the edges. On those occasions when I can remain still I can recall her rattling city buses, her green, well-tended parks, red brick mills, and corner taverns alongside corner churches. The rest is silence.

Mostly.

NOW...on the MOTION PICTURE SCREEN!

WALT DISNEY'S DAVY CROCKETT
KING OF THE WILD FRONTIER

STARRING
FESS PARKER
BUDDY EBSEN

Directed by NORMAN FOSTER
Written by TOM BLACKBURN
Produced by BILL WALSH

Adapted from the Original "Disneyland" Television Productions

COLOR BY TECHNICOLOR
WIDE SCREEN

Chapter 1

KING OF THE WILD FRONTIER

"You cannot smile a bear to death!"

"Didn't smile it, grinned it." Teddy replied.

"And he killed another bear when he was only three!" I added helpfully.

"A three year old cannot kill a bear! It's impossible!" Sometimes you could almost see steam coming out of Margaret Mary's ears when she was upset.

"Did too," Teddy said, "Says so in the song."

The voice of reason here is Margaret Mary Sullivan, pleading, well, shouting actually, as we stood in line to see "Davy Crockett, King of the Wild Frontier" outside the RKO Keith Theatre in Lowell, Massachusetts, on a beautiful Springtime Saturday morning many long years ago.

"We" is myself, Margaret Mary, (panting) and Teddy Gianoulous, my second best friend after Margaret Mary. All three of us were eight years old, bursting with excitement as we stood in line on the bubblegum spattered sidewalk leading into the theatre.

"Davy Crockett" was a big deal for us. We had been on our best behavior for weeks in order to see this movie. Me and Teddy were both wearing coon skin hats, much to the embarrassment of Margaret Mary, and though she would barely admit it, she was excited to see Davy too.

Looking back over the years it is hard to describe the frenzy we were caught up in with this Davy Crockett business. Originally telecast as a three part series on Walt Disney's wildly popular Sunday night television program, those wonderful folks at Disneyland simply cobbled together the three television episodes and released the whole shebang to the movie theatres as a feature film. Meanwhile Childhood America was inundated by Davy Crockett coonskin hats, shirts, pajamas, bedspreads, lunchboxes, trading cards, comics, plastic rifles, rubber knives, and I'm sure some long forgotten sugar drenched, Davy Crockett candy.

There was no escaping this mound of merchandising. Bigger than the Beatles, bigger than Elvis, almost as big as Santa Claus, Davy's theme song alone sold over ten million copies, more than any other record ever recorded to that time. To this very day Davy Crockett remains, by far, the most profitable franchise Disney has ever concocted. Quite simply, I didn't know a child our age who didn't know every word to the theme song, who hadn't been faithfully stationed in front of their TV set when Davy was originally broadcast, or who wasn't somewhere in this line, somewhere in the United States, to see this movie.

Incidentally, the RKO Keith theatre management wouldn't let kids in if they were chewing gum, which is why the sidewalk outside the lobby was polka dotted with pink, blue and disgusting black globs of crushed gum. Sneak chewers were expelled upon discovery by teenage ushers in red and gold blazers who prowled the darkened inside aisles with flashlights searching for any wrongdoing, like gum chewing. We barely noticed, we certainly didn't mind. We didn't have any chewing gum anyway. I'm not sure what the chewing gum policy was for adults, but for kids it was absolute, no gum, no admittance, no how.

My buddy Teddy was as blissfully satisfied with his facts coming from a song as Margaret Mary was when they came from the Encyclopedia Britannica or some other higher source of factdom. I was somewhere in the middle, though I was learning to lean towards Margaret Mary's higher sources, most of the time.

Margaret Mary, who in later years would become "Maggie" and even later, "Mags," a nick name she never fully embraced, was already a book and fact person who frequently filled the role of reality checker for Teddy and me. Teddy, truthfully, was far less concerned with having his reality checked than I was, an attitude far more appropriate for an eight year old awash in a sea of Cartoon

TV, comic books and Saturday morning movies as we were. At that age we rarely questioned what was told to us, quite content to believe, as fact, that Davy killed him a bear when he was only three, etcetera, etcetera, and etcetera.

Margaret Mary was, as yet, too young to be a full scale skeptic, but old enough and wise enough to research the facts surrounding much of the information being passed down to us. Eventually I would follow her down that road, but for now, that bright, sunny Saturday morning, I had all the facts I needed.

Killed him a bear when he was only three. Somehow.

Margaret Mary had entered my circle of life the year before, while I was in the third grade. She transferred into the Immaculate Conception school from Chicago where her father, Sean Patrick Sullivan, taught literature at Loyola University.

Margaret Mary's mother, Kathleen, had died the year before from a cancer that shattered their world. Lowell was meant to be a fresh start for father and daughter, free of the heartache of Kathleen's loss, though life would not work out that way. It seldom does.

But for this moment life was whole. I was in the moment, breathtakingly alive, quivering with anticipation and anchored by my two best friends. Let me tell you a little bit about them, and consequently more about my eight year old self.

Margaret Mary was bright as a candle, full of opinions and massively intolerant of willful ignorance. She came with the full-on Irish uniform, red hair, freckles and bright green eyes that would eventually transform from sparkling to piercing to enchanting. Margaret Mary was an old soul, who, since the death of her mother, had become caretaker for her tragically faltering father. She was then, and would remain, the smartest person I ever met, bright far beyond her years, kind far beyond her circumstance, good far beyond her limitations. She would be, for me, friend, mentor, companion and long lost love, taken far, far too soon from a world that desperately needed as many Margaret Mary's as there could be.

Her father, Sean, was a brilliant teacher, a gentle soul, a man of poetry and literature who counted Shakespeare, Keats and Mark Twain among his closest companions. After the death of his wife, Sean had taken to drink, moderately at first, but ongoing and intensifying as time moved forward. By the time they settled in Lowell Sean had forfeited his driver's license to the whiskey, and become becalmed in his sorrow, buoyed only by his fierce love and devotion to his daughter. Sean was often the adult arbiter of our confusion and the ultimate source for our youthful facts. Sometimes that was a good thing, other times, not so much.

Every Thursday night during the school year I would go to Margaret Mary's house to do homework after supper. Friday was test day at the Immaculate Conception school. Spelling and math, geography and history, religion and science all had to be accounted for before we could enjoy our weekends. Sean Patrick would hover nearby as we studied, ready as always to answer our questions or help us through a problem.

When we were finished studying he would read aloud to us from his beloved Keats and Hawthorne and Shakespeare. Most of the time I barely understood what he was reading, but the sound, the wonderful, rhythmic cadence of his words would never leave me. Later in life, long after he had joined Kathleen, I would hear his voice as I read from his favorites, now understanding the magic of the prose.

Sean Patrick Sullivan, Professor of English Literature at Lowell State Teachers College, widower of Kathleen Bernadette Sullivan, nee O'Malley, a sadly generous, brilliant, grieving man sinking into alcoholism, as the battered Irish often do.

Teddy Gianoulous, on the other hand, was my buddy, my baseball playing, comic book swapping, frog catching, bike riding, tree climbing, and puddle jumping amigo. Teddy lived next door to my family, another sorrowful child of a single parent. His mother too had passed away, though several years before. Teddy wasn't sure of what, his family did not speak of the circumstance. He was raised by his older sister, Connie, and his older brother, Chris. Connie was ten years older than Teddy, already out of high school and attending the Lowell Academy of Beauty, where she was studying to become a hair stylist. Connie was cheerful and friendly, de facto mother and homemaker to her brothers and father.

Teddy's brother, Chris, was a different kind of story. He was 19, surly, but very protective of Connie and Teddy. Chris was the first person I knew who rode a motorcycle, wore the legendary black leather jacket, dungarees, white t-shirt, with a pack of cigarettes rolled up in the sleeve, garrison boots and a glorious, shiny duck tail haircut held together by Brylcreem and frequent swipes of a pocket comb. Chris didn't talk much, he growled, but he kept a good eye on Teddy and Connie and, on the odd occasion, when he was in a good mood, would take us for rides on his motorcycle.

One day, in the unfolding years to come, Chris would disappear, motorcycle and all, over the hill and far away. Teddy believed he settled in Hollywood and became a stunt man in the movies. Teddy came to this conclusion because we had seen a movie called, "Merril's Marauders" and he swears he saw Chris in the movie, standing right behind a mule. I went to see the movie twice with Teddy and really didn't think so, but I never told Teddy that, he was my buddy.

Teddy's father, Nick, was generally considered to be the angriest man in Lowell. He was not mean, not cruel or abusive, just angry, not some of the time, all of the time. He owned a garage and worked seven days a week, dawn to dark. We would come to learn that he had been that way since the death of his wife. He provided food, clothing and shelter for his children but rarely spent any time with them. Perhaps if he had he would not have always been so angry.

Teddy would never be a book person. He didn't like school as much as Margaret Mary and I. In fact he didn't like school as much as anyone I knew, but Teddy could tell you the batting average of anybody on the Boston Red Sox and he could pull an inside fast ball clean out of the ballpark where we played our pick-up summer games. Teddy might not know Tom Sawyer from Tom Thumb but he could give you a pretty good explanation of why Superman could beat the crap out of Batman or even how to smile a bear to death.

Teddy was a good guy, my almost forever buddy until the river of time, adulthood and unseen circumstance separated us forever.

Mine was the family complete, mother, father and two younger brothers all under the same roof. We took our daily meals and slumber together, content and well cared for, at least on the surface. Sometimes, behind closed doors, my mother and father would argue, raised voices quickly hushed, with subsequent stony silences that went on for days. The issues themselves a mystery to my brothers and I, all the more terrifying for their obscurity. Then for no apparent reason we could know, the clouds of dissension between then would clear and we would be a happy family again, until the next time.

My Mom and Dad were two very different people, joined in the uncompromising Holy Matrimony of the day. I could see them only as parents, unaware and clueless as to their union as lovers, friends and fractionally functioning grown-ups struggling in the real world.

My Dad was a fine man, steady provider, role model for his three sons, teacher of sports and games, closet Santa Claus each Christmas and always, throughout my life my North Star, the point of moral reference I could point to and home in on as I moved forward in my life's journey.

My Mother was a woman of great beauty, though afflicted by a sadness she could never define. She was prone to tears we could not understand, bereft at most times of joy, and possessed by a disparagement she often shared with her children. When she was happy, we were happy as well, though her more common unhappiness could stain the brightest of our days.

One thing I was ever sure of throughout my childhood and on into my adult years, was that each of them, my Mom and Dad, always did the best they could for me and my brothers and for themselves within the limitations of their secret selves.

As children we were, all three of us, defined by our families, molded, modeled, educated and in some cases damaged by them. What they were, we would become, leavened by outside influences, our schooling, our companions, and for the first time ever, our third parent, our most influential influencer, the TV.

That glowing silver light in the living room, entertainer, babysitter, source of reward, bringer of magic, salesman of superficiality, the beloved, immortal, essential, diabolical TV.

Here is where we first met Davy Crockett, Mickey Mouse, Ozzie and Harriet, The Honeymooners, Captain Kangaroo and Captain Midnight. TV is where we found our heroes, our villains, our sinners and our saints, beamed straight into our living room and our heads every night till bedtime and every Saturday morning.

Movies were important too of course, gigantic, wide screened, Technicolor dreams of romance and adventure glowing up there on the giant screen, in the wonderful, magical darkness of the movie theatre. Movies were colossal TV, double features of fantasy, but they cost money, and you had to go down city to see them. TV was right in our own home, right in the living room, there where we lived, a part of the family, part of our brain. In later years, just a very few actually, another outside voice would live between my ears, shape my thoughts and feed my moods.

The thumping, driving, foot stomping rhythm of rock and roll would come along and sweep my generation along with it. But rock and roll is for later as are so many other distractions.

Meanwhile back at the Saturday morning gum spattered sidewalk, the movie line mercifully started inching forward to where Mr. Desmond, who managed the theatre, stood at a little wooden stand taking tickets, tearing them in half, and handing one of the pieces back before we could go into the theatre. He also checked to see if we were chewing gum.

That hurdle passed, we glided into the coolness of the lobby and into the most mouth-watering, flavorful cloud of warm and buttery popcorn scented air on earth. Avalanches of puffy white popcorn spilled out of a brass kettle into a glass booth right before our eyes. Mounded in snow like drifts the toasty popcorn was scooped into striped paper bags and sold for a nickel a piece, to anyone who had an extra nickel. Alongside the popcorn machine, plump pink hot dogs rotated on metal skewers as they were "Radiant Cooked" on the snack bar countertop.

Moist and fragrant buns were steamed alongside the cooker and below, apparently shielded from the radiant heat, were rows and stacks of bags and boxes of Junior Mints, Sugar Babies, Spice Drops, Sky Bars, Licorice Sticks, Cinnamon Dots, Necco Wafers, Three Musketeer bars and Bit O' Honey candies. No gum.

Mrs. Desmond, aproned and smiling, dispensed the treats to the more affluent children as we three averted our eyes and breathed the popcorn flavored air as little as possible, our immediate funds exhausted by the movie tickets.

The minute we were safely past the candy counter Teddy took off like a rocket to find us the best seats. Margaret Mary took my hand as she often did when we were swept up in a crowd. After all these years I still recall how wonderful this made me feel. Davy Crockett may have killed him a bear when he was only three, but I could make Margaret Mary feel a little more secure in a swirling crowd by holding her hand. Take that Mr. Crockett.

Amidst the bedlam we walked together up the carpeted ramp that led into the theatre where we could see Teddy waving frantically from one of the middle rows. The theatre was still brightly lit as seats filled fast with hundreds of kids screeching with joy and anticipation, waiting for the lights to dim and the magic to begin.

We settled in next to Teddy and as you probably know, in short order Davy had captured Red Stick, gone to Congress, patched up the crack in the Liberty Bell and fought alongside Jim Bowie and Buck Travis at the Alamo. Teddy, Margaret Mary and I sat stock still through every note of the closing credit theme song before we filed slowly out of the theatre, sodden with satisfaction, to squint into the bright midday sunshine.

Regrouping on the gum spattered sidewalk, Teddy already had his theories.

"You know, maybe Davy didn't get killed. He coulda' got away." Teddy announced hopefully.

"Yeah, they didn't show him getting killed." I added.

"Everybody at the Alamo was killed, all the defenders anyway. I looked it up at the library." Margaret Mary replied, a hint of sadness in her voice.

"If everybody got killed, who wrote down that everybody got killed?"

I always loved Teddy's leaps of logic.

"Mrs. Almeron Dickinson, her baby daughter and a slave named Jim lived. They told everybody what happened." Margaret Mary, quoting from her beloved encyclopedia once again.

"Those guys weren't even in the movie!" Teddy proclaimed, dismissing Margaret Mary and her encyclopedia.

"That doesn't mean they weren't at the Alamo, Teddy, just that they weren't in the movie." Again I heard a hint of sadness in Margaret Mary's voice. Then she brightened and announced, "My father said to meet him at Brighams. He said we could have ice cream." Davy's mortality momentarily forgotten, we set off at a determined pace for the ice cream parlor.

Most Saturday mornings Sean Patrick would ride with us on the bus to downtown Lowell, called "down city" by the native folk, and deposit us at a movie theatre, either the Keith or the Strand, sometimes the Rialto, and then repair to the Lowell Public Library. While we dreamed our movie dreams, he dreamed his among the wonderful musty smelling stacks of books and magazines and newspapers of the library reading room. Books were where Sean Patrick went to escape from his realities as we did with our movies and though the memory of his wife's death hung on him like a shroud, he tried monstrously hard to be the best father he could to Margaret Mary. Today that included meeting us at the ice cream parlor.

Separating ourselves from the herd of children outside the movie theatre we headed for Brigham's Tea Room and Ice Cream parlor in Kearney Square. Brighams was the go-to eatery in downtown Lowell. Sparkling clean and shiny, Brighams had an elegant, marble topped soda fountain with eight red topped, spinning stools at the counter and tiny tables with real linen tablecloths scattered throughout the dining room. There were six high backed booths along the walls with red upholstery and Formica tabletops. They liked the kids to sit in the booths. Less wear and tear on the linens. We slid into a booth and placed our ice cream orders as the Davy Crockett conversation resumed. Margaret Mary patiently rolled her eyes and sighed.

"He could have jumped over the wall and got away." Teddy decided, hoping for some reassurance.

"Yeah, all the Mexican guys were running into the Alamo, he could have waited till they all got inside, then jumped over the wall and got away outside." Warped as this sounds today, right then it made sense to me, at least until I saw the expression on Margaret Mary's face.

"Davy Crockett died at the Alamo. It says so in all the history books." Margaret Mary was gently trying to lead us down a path to common sense that Teddy and I were not quite ready to follow just yet.

"Well, still maybe he could have gotten away." I decided, just as our ice cream arrived.

Brighams had the best ice cream, made fresh at a local dairy and served in tulip shaped metal cups, three generous scoops for twenty-five cents. The large glass of water, chock full of crystal clear ice, was free. We dug in, leaving Davy's fate to be decided later. Half-way through our ice cream Sean Patrick arrived, smiling and happy, a book of poetry under his arm and a hint of brandy in his eyes.

"How was the movie kiddo's? Has virtue triumphed and all good deeds rewarded?"

"We think maybe Davy Crockett could have got away and not got killed at the Alamo." Teddy declared.

"Ah, Crockett, a broth of an Irishman I'm sure. Perhaps the paddy luck was with him. Who's to say?" Sean Patrick slid into the booth next to Margaret Mary, kissing her atop her head as he settled in.

Margaret Mary, with considerable effort, said nothing. Sean ordered coffee which he sipped with elegance and grace as we chattered happily about the movie and how we should spend the rest of our day. Plans decided and ice cream finished, we headed for the bus stop. Teddy started humming Davy's theme song, I joined in. Margaret Mary walked ahead of us with her father. Not humming.

I have revisited this wondrous morning many times over my aged years longing to recapture the sense of happiness, the joy, the anticipation of these moments, that magical Saturday morning so very long ago. Nothing in my today days seems to come close and I do miss it so. The flavor of those years is best experienced through my family's store of grainy black and white, 8mm movie film. Herky-jerky, almost stop action movements of family ghosts long past, beam from the screen, smiling and happy, filled with hope and assurance that their present was the best of times and their future sure to be better and better, though life would not work out that way, it seldom does.

As the years rolled by and facts replaced fiction, we learned that Davy had indeed died at the Alamo, that the heroic fight for independence had actually been part of a massive land grab intended to steal Texas from Mexico, and that, rather than freedom, the Texans in revolt were also motivated by the desire to keep their slaves, an institution Mexico had outlawed years before. Such were the sordid details of history, carefully obscured in our comic book world.

As we bounced along on the Oakland's bus to Belvedere I stared out the window at all the familiar street signs, store fronts, neatly aligned houses and landmarks along the way never realizing how deeply ingrained into my genetic crust these sights and sounds and smells would soak and slumber and remain with me for all my days. Kil't him a bear when he was only three. Somehow.

There would be many more Saturday mornings, not all as magical as this one, but formative all the same, shaping me into the person I am today. What I miss most is the simplicity, the innocence from the facts, the nitty gritty, the real deal. Back then we could be smart without being hip, unhindered by unrelenting reality, unaware that such bliss can only be fleeting. More growing up to do on the journey.

ONWARD.

"Cinema is the most beautiful fraud in the whole world."

Jean-Luc Godard

When I was a child, I spoke as a child, I understood as a child, I thought as a child, but when I became a man, I put away childish things

1.   Corinthians 13:11

But Not Yes!

Chapter 2

NOT SO LITTLE LEAGUE

It was another almost summer Saturday morning in May, one school year after the Davy Crockett frenzy had died down. Dozens of kids like Teddy and me are arriving at Shedd Park, to the Little League baseball diamond, for tryout day. In today's Politically Correct Wonderland every one of us would make a team, but not then, not at these tryouts. Each team could have fifteen kids. Six teams, most had eight or nine players back from last year. There were about forty of us trying out. Some would be chosen, the rest rejected, in the newspaper no less, when the six Little League team's rosters were announced.

Ninety boys could play, the rest, not so much. Half of us were not going to be chosen. Little League selection in this period was brutal, survival of the fittest, mostly.

"I hope we do good today" Teddy said as we rode our bikes to the ball field. "Me too," I answered, trying to keep the shake out of my voice.

"I'd hate it if we don't get picked", Teddy added, "When Richie Meehan didn't get picked last year he threw up."

It didn't necessarily make me any less nervous to have Teddy remind me why I had tossed and turned most of last night, and been too nervous to eat breakfast this morning, but he was right. This was it. The first big sorting of our lives, into haves and have nots, Little League style, was waiting for us at our favorite playground on this fateful, frightening Saturday morning. I didn't answer Teddy, just gulped back the lump in my throat and peddled on.

"I hope I get the Red Sox," Teddy continued, oblivious to my rapidly growing anxiety, "but any team will do except the Yankees."

That was Teddy, concerned only with which team he'd play on while I would be glad, thrilled, to be on any team at all.

"Wow!" Teddy exclaimed as we came in sight of the field, "Look at all the people! I didn't think this many people would be here. Did you?"

So far Teddy was doing an aces job of keeping my fear factor at the highest level possible. There were an awful lot of people clustered around the Little League field.

"No way", was all I could muster in response, "Maybe they're waiting here for something else to happen." I hoped.

"Nah, they're here for the tryouts alright, there's Mike's mother and father and Steve's."

They were there all right. Things were getting scarier by the minute. Yet as intimidating as the crowd was, as nervous as I was, the sight of the bright and shiny field dazzled me. After a long and cold, icy and snowy winter, after the mud and slush of early spring, the emerald green grass and meticulously engraved dimensions of the ballpark raised my spirits and for just that first moment the knot in my belly and the lump in my throat disappeared. The infield grass had been freshly cut, manicured is the word that comes to mind, by Mr. Rayburn, the park's caretaker. Fresh white chalk marked the pristine foul lines and batter's boxes, the pitcher's mound and base paths had been raked smooth, the outfield shimmered like a mountain meadow and the air itself felt as if it had been scrubbed clean for today's events. To this day there are not many things I find as reassuring, as comforting as a freshly groomed ball field. Teddy and I both stopped and stared and I calmed down, just a little bit, as we waited for the tryouts to begin. But the longer we waited the more wobbly my knees felt.

Moms and Dads were scattered about the edges of the field offering encouragement to their children, chatting with neighbors, minding the younger folk. My father was going to stop by after he got the oil changed in his car and dropped my mother off at her sister's. I knew he would be cheering for me to do well. I hoped, hoped, hoped I would not disappoint him.

In the meantime dogs barked and frolicked, birds sang in the trees, clouds floated lazily by and, on the ten foot flagpole in center field, our 48 star flag waved proudly against the clear blue panorama of the springtime sky.

Little League baseball in my hometown back in the day was a vital first step on the road to distinction, recognition, even virtue. Kids who were on the teams were respected, part of a very particular "in" crowd. The ones who didn't make a team, well, they had to swallow that bitter pill and find some other way to be well thought of.

Games were played at 6 o'clock, on warm summer nights, to crowds of proud parents and grandparents, aunts, uncles and giggling young girls who were only just beginning to distract the ballplayers.

Eventually Teddy and I were called over to where the coaches of the six teams were chatting with some of the parents, checking paperwork, and pinning large paper numbers onto the shirts of we hopefuls. Some of the older kids, already on teams were over there as well, wearing their uniform shirt or hat and strutting about like peacocks. My heart ached to be one of them. Freshly numbered we joined the other kids and waited some more.

Most of the grown-ups had now gathered behind the backstop at home plate or in the rickety green stands along the third base line, but out beyond the left field fence, on the dirt track which ran to the tennis courts we could see Teddy's brother, Chris, sitting on his motorcycle, smoking a cigarette. When I saw him I pointed him out to Teddy. Teddy waved. Chris just kept smoking, and watching. "Chris don't like bunches of people." Teddy said, shifting his gaze from his brother to the crowd around home plate. I couldn't think of a lot of things Chris did like, but I didn't say that to Teddy, he was my buddy.

No Margaret Mary this day. Baseball was strictly guy stuff. She would be home with her Dad, a book each on comfortable front porch chairs no doubt. Margaret Mary's father had a theory about sports, "Let the boyos jump about, best to leave them alone while they are sporting." Margaret Mary couldn't have agreed more.

In fact, and you can't make this stuff up, girls were not allowed to play Little League baseball, or any organized baseball at all during this period. The first girl to play in the Little League clipped her pigtails, dressed like a boy, tried out, made the team in the Dairy Little League of Corning, New York in 1951. She played first base under the nickname, I swear, "Tubby". Of course the ruse was soon discovered, Tubby revealed to be nine year old Kay Johnston, and the scandal broke far and wide. Her coach, to his everlasting credit, stated she was "a damn good ballplayer" and would remain on the team the rest of the season. The League however banned her and subsequently passed a rule, I swear to God, called, "The Tubby Rule" which officially forbade girls from playing in the Little League. This marvelous piece of legislation would stand unchallenged for twenty three years. Girls were not officially allowed to play until 1974 when one courageous young lady lawyered up. Life marches on, but that road behind looks bumpier all the time.

"Okay, everybody gather around." A guy with a clipboard announced. After making sure we all had a number, he introduced himself as Jerry Derosier. He was the head umpire of the Little League and would be in charge that day. We could call him Mr. Derosier.

"When I call your number I want you to take the field and run out to the position you are trying out for. Each of you will get three grounders and three pop ups. Stay at your position until everyone has their turn, then hustle off. You'll get a chance to bat when the fielding is over. Everybody understand?"

With that same old huge lump in my throat and a basketball sized chunk of ice in my belly I nodded along with the rest of the boys. We understood. Somewhat to my relief most everyone else looked just as nervous as I felt. We were instructed to sit along the third base sideline, back from the field and wait our turn. Teddy and I plopped down on the new mowed lawn amidst the other boys. There wasn't much conversation among us, and it was hard to look the other boys in the eye. Teddy offered me a piece of gum, "Double Bubble". Double Bubble Gum was sweet and good, chewing was good, and it made the waiting easier, a little. I thanked Teddy with a nervous nod and pounded on my glove, bouncing off invisible walls as we sat in the grass. Just another great thing about Baseball, it allowed gum.

Baseball had been a constant in my life, my earliest passion, ever since my father had taken me out on the front lawn when I was five years old and taught me how to play catch. He had been a ballplayer as a young man, forsaking the game only when holding two jobs, having three sons and attending night school had overtaxed his fervor for the game. It was however a fervor he passed on to me and spring and summer would always be, above all else, baseball season to me. Besides playing catch, and teaching me to swing a bat, run the bases, gather in pop-ups and grounders my Dad shared with me the wonders of the sports pages, game recaps and box scores, fascinations which have also remained with me to this day. The love of Baseball runs deep in my soul and here I was, nine years old and about to take the field to find out if I was good enough for one of those six exalted, and highly selective, Little League teams.

Teddy was in the first group called. He ran to the outfield and caught all three fly balls hit to him. Teddy had a good arm and fired the ball back in on a line. I stood up and cheered for him when he came in. He had a big smile on his face and I was glad he had done well. But feeling glad for Teddy didn't make me any less nervous when I heard my number called.

"They're hitting 'em easy," Teddy offered. "Don't sweat it."

Pounding my glove I ran out to third base. Once everyone was in position one of the coaches pointed at me and said, "Heads up third base, make a clean throw over to first."

And then the sky fell in. The first grounder went right through my legs. I took my eye off the ball and by me it rolled. I turned beet red and awash with shame. I caught the second grounder but bounced the throw over to first because I hurried it and didn't plant my feet the way my Dad had showed me a hundred times. The third grounder clanked off my glove and rolled into foul territory. The batter made kind of a face and pointed at the shortstop. He hit him a ground ball as I tried with all my might to stand there and not cry.

After he hit grounders to the rest of the infielders the batter pointed at me again and lifted a pop up toward third base. I got under it and made a clean catch and fired it back in. He said "again" and hit one a little further away from me. I caught this one too and after I fired it back in I saw my dad smiling at me from the sidelines. The batter then pointed at the shortstop and said, "Heads up" and hit him a pop fly. I thought I was supposed to get three. The rest of the guys only got two as well, unless they dropped one, then they got another chance. When we all had our turn we ran off the field and waited for our turn to bat. I wondered if my Dad had seen me mess up the grounders and I still felt a little sick to my stomach as I walked over to him. My Dad had come over and put his arm around my shoulders.

"Nice goin' on the pop-ups," he said. How'd you do on the grounders?"

"Not so good," I missed two of them."

"Well you looked good out there, wait till you get your turn at bat. You'll show 'em." Dad gave me a squeeze and a smile and I felt better than I had all morning.

Teddy pounded the ball when he got up. He yanked one right over the fence in left field and I saw all the coaches nodding their heads and writing on their clip boards. I knew Teddy had it made and I was happy for him. Then they called my number again and the pain in my stomach returned.

"You can do this, Son," my Dad said, "Just keep your eye on the ball and swing level, not hard. It doesn't have to go out of the park. Just make contact, you'll be fine."

And I was. I hit all five balls they threw me. One hit the fence on a bounce, not as far as Teddy's, but close. The rest were good hits too, liners and a sharp ground ball. I felt better when I stepped away from the plate. My Dad was smiling at me too. Out beyond left field we heard the sound of Chris' motorcycle roaring away.

When everybody had their ups Mr. Derosier called all us kids together and thanked us for trying out. He said the results would be in the newspaper next Friday and that if we didn't make a team this year he hoped we would come back next year and try again.

After that everybody started to drift away but I saw my Dad over talking to Mr. Derosier. They seemed to know each other and I saw Mr. Derosier look over at me and make a mark on his clipboard. I hoped that meant something good.

After the tryouts we went down to Lefty's Drive In for a snack, our bikes packed snugly into the back of my Dad's station wagon. Tucked into a corner table at Lefty's Teddy and I demolished our hot dogs in record time and slurped happily on our cokes while my Dad drank coffee and grinned at us.

"You two act like you haven't eaten in a week." Dad said as he turned to Anthony behind the counter. "Two more hot dogs over here, Tony. These guys look like they're starving."

"Do ya think we did good, Mr. Ferrier?" Teddy asked, "I mean like compared to the other guys?"

"You did fine, both of you did fine. Now it's up to the coaches to realize how well you did. I'm sure you'll both make teams," and then he hesitated and leaned forward on the table, "but even if you don't keep in mind that you did your best. You showed up and tried out and made the effort. The rest isn't up to you. I'm proud of you both for being there."

The slowest, most painful week of my up-to-then life crawled by while I waited for the Friday night newspaper. Then it was there, in black and white on the bottom left corner of the Sports page, "Rosters Announced for Shedd Park Little League." My hands were shaking and I had forgotten how to breathe as I scanned the clusters of names under each team's banner. Teddy made the Cubs.

I passed over the Indians, Braves, Pirates, Yankees, and there it was. I made the Red Sox! Said so in the paper! My Dad wasn't home from work yet so I tore out of my house with the paper to find Teddy. He was in his driveway watching Chris tinker with his motorcycle.

"Teddy! We made it! You're on the Cubs! I'm a Red Sox!"

Teddy turned around with a giant smile. Even Chris smiled a little and put down his wrench. He wiped his hands on a rag and ruffled up Teddy's hair as he went into the house. He even smiled at me which he hardly ever did "Good going guys." He offered.
Teddy and I scanned the paper again, making sure our names were still there, seeing who else had made the teams. I couldn't wait for my Dad to get home so I could tell him. Teddy and I couldn't stop grinning. We could have grinned a bear to death.

Life should always be that good on the journey.

ONWARD.

"BASEBALL IS LIKE CHURCH. MANY ATTEND, FEW UNDERSTAND."

Leo Durocher

Chapter 3

FADDA MURPHY

"Fadda Murphy, Fadda Murphy!" Peter Rayburn squeaked frantically, waving his hand from his school desk.

At the front of the classroom Father Daniel Murphy, OMI, resignedly halted his lesson and prepared himself for Peter's latest assault on Scripture. He nodded his kindly white haired head at Peter, who rose to stand respectfully beside his desk with his urgent question.

"Fadda, if Adam and Eve only had two kids, and Cain killed Abel, who was his bruddah, where did everyone else come from when Adam and Eve died?"

Before Father Murphy could answer, Sister Evangelina, the sixth grade class's primary teacher, rose from her seat in the back of the classroom and stomped toward Peter.

"I'll answer that for you Father." Pinching Peter by the ear she led him out of the classroom to the dreaded solitary confinement of the cloakroom. Taking a deep breath of relief Father Murphy reopened his New Testament storybook and resumed reading to us about the Miracle of the Loaves and Fishes.

This is Christian Doctrine Class, also known as Catechism, Immaculate Conception School, Sixth Grade style, Lowell, Massachusetts in the Year of Our Lord, 1959.

The first thing you have to know about this tale is that Peter Rayburn didn't actually talk that way. He put on the accent only to annoy the hierarchy, which he did quite well. Peter was the only son of Mr. Rayburn, the head groundskeeper at Shedd Park and Doris Rayburn, his long suffering and amazingly tolerant mother. Peter and his Dad had a unique, but thorny relationship which resulted in their being known as "Hey" for Mr. Rayburn and "Hey Jr." for Peter. "Hey" is how they addressed each other in daily communion at the Park, Mr.

Rayburn as he went about his grounds keeping duties, and Peter as one of our neighborhood playmates.

Unlike Margaret Mary, who embraced knowledge as her birthright, Peter saw knowledge as a weapon, a challenge to all that authority that hovered over us. Peter was a bright kid, though he researched rather than read, and to his discredit his insights eventually soured to sarcasm as the years rolled on, a not uncommon occurrence in our festering, stagnant hometown.

I always admired Peter's fearlessness in confronting those authority figures, asking the difficult, if somewhat strange questions and not giving in until giving in was all there was left to do. Peter was the only person I ever knew who underlined parts of the Bible that made no sense to him and openly, repeatedly, consistently questioned the goings on within whenever he could confront an advocate. Peter did a lot, a whole lot, of underlining.

"You shouldn't embarrass Father Murphy like that," Margaret Mary said as we walked home from school that day. Peter didn't answer, he shrugged off Margaret Mary's criticism as easily as he shrugged off his penitent cloak room time.

In the resulting silence I was suddenly struck by a thought.

"Buffaloes. I was thinking about buffaloes." I added genuinely puzzled.

"What about buffaloes?" Margaret Mary asked.

"Well, last week they told us buffaloes were only found in North America right?"

Margaret Mary nodded in agreement, cautiously.

"Well if you could only get buffaloes in North America and nobody even knew where North America was until like a thousand years later, how did Noah get two buffaloes to go in the Ark?"

Peter's line of inquiry was getting contagious.

"God knew where North America was. He could have brought two buffaloes to where Noah was building the Ark." Margaret Mary responded.

"Doesn't say anything about that in the Bible," Peter noted. "I looked it up."

"When you can't figure some things out you have to have faith to understand. That's what religion is, having faith." Margaret Mary explained.

By now our walk home from school had halted by a park bench at Shedd Park as the discussion continued.

"And how come God made a big flood that killed everybody that he didn't like?" I mean like he killed little babies and all the dogs and cats and old people. Why couldn't he have just disappeared all the bad guys and let everybody else live?" Genuine anger crept into Peter's voice as he tossed his books onto the bench.

Margaret Mary was strangely silent. I was wondering about penguins, God must have gone and got them for Noah too. Peter's indignation was unabated.

"You know what Sister Angelina told me in the cloakroom? She said I had a sin on my soul for asking Bad questions to Father Murphy and that I should tell it in confession for forgiveness. I mean, now it's a sin to ask questions?"

As Peter stomped and Mary Margaret pondered, my head was full of pictures of God drowning my Grandfather and Grandmother because he didn't like what some other people had done. I had never, ever even seen my grandparents get mad at anything or anybody. These leaps of faith were getting bigger all the time.

"Hi Guys", Teddy sang out as he joined us at the bench. Teddy didn't go to the Immaculate Conception School with us. His father went to the Greek Orthodox Church, sometime, and Teddy didn't go to any church at all, rendering him oblivious to the mysteries of Catholic dogma. Teddy attended "public school", an institution the Gray Nuns of the Sacred Heart, who taught at the Immaculate Conception, assured us was inferior in every way to the education we were receiving.

"Didja hear about Richie Burke? Butchie Martin clobbered him after school for looking at his sister." Teddy announced.

"They had a fight because somebody looked at somebody else's sister?" Margaret Mary asked indignantly.

"I think maybe he said something too, I don't know. Wasn't much of a fight though, Butchie clobbered him."

"I would'na messed with Butchie." Peter added, "Butchie fights good."

"Yeah, remember when he beat up that kid from over at O"Donnell Park for spitting on his bike?" Teddy added.

"I wouldn't spit on Butchie's bike for anything." I added.

"Why would ANYBODY spit on anybody's bike?" Margaret Mary asked, her exasperation peaking.

"I spit on a guy once playing basketball," Teddy offered, "but it was an accident."

"That the guy you got in a fight with over at Gormly Field?" I asked.

"Yeah, he spit back and it wasn't an accident."

"Spit fight or a real fight?" Peter asked.

"There's such a thing as a spit fight?" Margaret Mary was clearly horrified.

"Spit fights are for little kids." I explained. "Butchie Martin don't ever spit fight."

"I'm going home," Margaret Mary announced. There was an exasperation limit for Margaret Mary. Some days we hit it faster than others.

After Margaret Mary left, Peter, Teddy and I hung around our park bench while waiting for the rest of our gang to arrive.

"Hey Teddy, you ever read the Bible or any stuff like that?" Peter asked.

"Nah, my father says that's all a bunch of make believe stuff that priests use to make us give them money."

"Your father said that?" I was amazed, even a little frightened to hear such a thing.

"Yeah, but he don't talk about it much. He said it makes people mad if you do."

"I think it's the neatest thing I ever heard a grown up say." Peter answered. "If I ever said something like that I'd spend the rest of my life in the cloak room."

"And then you'd go to hell." I added.

"My father says there ain't no hell," Teddy added, "Or heaven either. He says all that stuff is made up."

This literally stunned me speechless. In all my life I had never heard such a thing. Heaven and hell made up? Why would anybody think such a thing?

"You mean your father don't believe in God?" Peter's question was filled with wonder and, I suspect, a little bit of respect.

"He said once that if there was a God he wouldn'ta let my mother die. But Chris told me that my Dad had too much to drink that night. I ain't never heard him say anything like that again."

"Yeah, but he said it, and he don't make you go to church or nothin'." Peter replied,

"He says he's got better things to do, but we can go by ourselves if we want to. I guess I don't want to."

I was still too shocked to speak. No God? No church? I was looking at Teddy an entirely different way now, he was either smarter than me, or he was going to hell. I sure didn't want to think of Teddy as burning forever in hell. Like myself, Peter had grown quiet, reviewing his options most likely.

For all his skeptical questioning of the Bible and our religious upbringing I'm sure that, like myself, he had never contemplated outright disbelief before.

"You guys aren't mad at me are you?" Teddy asked.

"I'm not mad Teddy," I answered quickly, "I just never heard nobody say they didn't believe in God before."

"I didn't say I didn't believe in God. I said my father didn't believe in God."

"So do you?' Peter asked, "Do you believe in God?"

"I guess so, I just don't think about it that much."

"But like, don't you pray for stuff?" I was still bewildered by this whole concept.

"Nah, my father says praying for stuff to happen is a waste of time."

Yet I had prayed for things many times, and many times my prayers had been answered. I prayed that I would make the Little League, and I did. I prayed that I would pass many a test, and I had. I prayed I wouldn't drown when I went swimming and I never drowned. When I was younger my Mother would come to my bedside every night and we would say a prayer that I wouldn't die in my sleep that night, and I didn't. I prayed all the time for things to happen, or not happen, and mostly my prayers seemed to work. Yet I couldn't help but wonder if some of the other kids who had tried out for Little League had prayed they would make it too, but they didn't. In my ten year old head I reasoned that some people pray better than others, or are more worthy in God's eyes, and that was why some people's prayers didn't come true.

In later years I would come to consider that my habit of crediting prayer for life's accomplishments robbed me of much needed self-esteem and personal pride for those childhood successes I earned. Praying to pass a test in school discounted my efforts at studying and being selected for Little League or any other sport team had more to do with my performance than supplication. By the time I realized I could accomplish things on my own I had barnacles on my knees. However those insights were many years in the future as I look back on that after school afternoon at Shedd Park.

"Don't cha' ever pray for anything, Teddy?" I finally managed to ask.

"Nah, but sometimes I pray to my mother, just so I can like talk to her."

Neither Peter nor I had any response to that, but the big question had now been raised and I couldn't get it out of my head. "Hey guys," Teddy pleaded, "Don't tell anybody about this stuff okay? I don't wanna' get my father in trouble or nuthin'."

Peter and I both promised but inside I knew this was something I was going to have to have a long talk about with Margaret Mary, the smartest person I knew.

That evening, after supper, I went over to Margaret Mary's house. She was surprised to see me because it wasn't the night before tests night and we didn't have a lot of other homework. I must have looked upset and I couldn't fool Margaret Mary for a minute when I was.

"What's the matter?" She asked, swinging wide her back porch door to let me in. "Is something wrong?"

"Kind'a, Teddy told me something today but I'm not supposed to tell anybody about it."

Of course from that exact second Margaret Mary had me telling the whole story. I felt bad about promising Teddy, but Margaret Mary promised not to tell anyone if I told her and I was sure she had more character than me.

"People like that are called atheists," she explained. "They used to be called heretics and they were burned at the stake, of course they don't do that anymore."

"What do they do to them?" I was almost afraid to ask.

"They don't do anything to them, but I'm pretty sure they all go to hell."

'And just who is going to hell on this very fine Tuesday evening?" Sean Patrick asked as he joined us on the back porch.

"Atheists. I was saying I think they all go to hell."

"I wouldn't be so sure, Margaret Mary," Sean answered, seating himself on one of the comfortable porch chairs. "Don't you think it's possible for a man, or woman, who has led a good life, a kind life, to go to heaven even if he or she does not believe there is one?"

"But the nuns said if you don't believe in God you can't go to heaven." I replied.

"Ah, the Sisters, Brides of Christ that they are, may not be the final authority on who goes to heaven or not."

Now Sean had our full attention. Positioning ourselves on the porch glider Margaret Mary and I were brim full of questions.

It was only two years before, on this very same porch that we three had sat here as Sean gently explained the whole Santa Claus situation to me. I had heard a rumor around the schoolyard regarding Santa being bogus and was surprised to find that Margaret Mary was reluctant to talk about it. After considerable badgering on my part she suggested I come to her house that night and we could talk about it with her father. He then kind-heartedly told me that it was my parents who were my true Christmas benefactors and that all the stories of elves and flying reindeer and bags of presents from the North Pole were made up stories for little children.

Dumbfounded as I was, I sat there, with Margaret Mary holding my hand, as Sean explained that gifts on Christmas were a way of celebrating the birth of Baby Jesus and that Santa Claus was a way to show how the gifts got under the Christmas tree. He went on to say we should not be telling other children about this because it was best to let them believe in Santa Claus as long as they could. Knowing the truth about Santa Claus, he explained, was part of growing up, and keeping the secret was a sort of pact with other grown-ups to keep Christmas special. Of course all this was more than a bit much to take in and I was immediately worried that this might hinder the flow of my presents. Assured that it would not, I agreed to the deal, even then I had my priorities.

Later Margaret Mary told me she had known about the whole Santa Claus fable for some time but had thought it best not to tell me. I wondered what else Margaret Mary knew that she had not told me and I wondered how much more of what I was being told would turn out to be tales told to children.

"Sister Evangelina told us that unless you believed in Jesus you would go to hell." Margaret Mary stated emphatically. "She said that Jesus came down from Heaven to save us all from Original Sin but if we didn't believe in him we would burn in hell forever. Right?"

Margaret Mary was looking at me for agreement and I was dutifully nodding my head in full support. Sean Patrick drew a very deep breath and leaned forward in his chair.

"You will have many questions regarding your Catholic faith in the years to come, best you take them slow and rely on the good intentions of the Church as you go along."

"But all that stuff is true right? About heaven and hell and all that?" I couldn't help but ask.

"True as we can expect to know in this life, for as far as I can recall not a soul has come back to tell us if indeed heaven awaits" Sean answered, then deftly tried to change the subject, "But aren't you two having some homework to consider this evening?"

There was no way Margaret Mary was going to let go of this subject yet.

You have to understand that by this time we had been given a boat load of Scripture, Gospels, Commandments and Dogma, as well as multiple homilies and horror stories, all filtered through the prism of Catholicism. We knew all about Original Sin, Mortal Sin, Venial Sin, Fasting, Abstinence, Penance, and the horrible implications of trifling with such doings. Let me give you an example or two.

By the time we had entered third grade, making us 10 years old or so, we were to begin preparing for our First Holy Communion. This is one of the primary sacraments of the Catholic Church through which fledgling Catholics, like ourselves, would receive the Body and Blood of Christ into our bodies. This concept was quite difficult to get one's head around, particularly if you were in the third grade, but receive it we would, only after we had been purged of all of our sins. Our third grade, ten year old sins.

The Catholic Church has a ritual called Confession in which you go to your church, enter a darkened booth and confess to a priest all of the sins which are staining your soul. The BIG sins, called Mortal Sins, which, if you died with ONE on your soul, meant you would burn in hell forever, consisted of all the majors, murder, rape, robbery, arson and the like, but there were others, equally grievous, which also condemned you to the Pit and were more within the capabilities of ten year olds.

Eating meat on Friday was one, any meat, for any reason. Hell, fire and damnation, forever. Just like murder, rape and robbery, only without the clear cut definition of why such an act was wrong. It was, period.

Swearing, was yet another trip to hellfire, though there were big swears (mortal sins) and little swears, (venial sins). The four letter synonym for fornication, was a big swear, Mortal Sin, hell, forever, while the four letter substitute for feces was a Venial Sin, no hell, but an unspecified stint in Purgatory, kind of like Hell Light, with a release date.

Lying and stealing could be either Mortal or Venial, depending on either the dollar amount or the subject matter. Stealing a penny candy was, as I recall, a venial sin, while stealing a nickel candy bar could be a mortal sin. Lying could be venial, there were "little white lies" and big lies, usually connected to a felony, though highly unlikely for a ten year old. Things got complicated when there were compound sins, lying about stealing for example, or eating meat on Friday and then lying about it. Sins were in fact myriad and multiple, frighteningly inevitable consequences of everyday behavior which hung over our lives like a deadly rainstorm.

"Listen, my children", as gently as I ever recall an adult speaking to me, Sean Patrick Sullivan implored, "Much of what you have been taught, and even more of what you have been told will change and turn as the years roll by." Sean's voice filled with a sadness, a melancholy blessed and cursed of the Irish as he continued, "Childhood fables about sinners and saints are created to ease the way for you to a much more harsh and unforgiving world. Try to remember that within those tales lies a lesson and that lesson may help you to face what lies ahead. I cannot answer all those things that you want to know but I will try, as best I can to be honest with you about the differences between what you are being taught and what I believe to be true."

"Sister Evangelina told Peter Rayburn it was a sin to ask questions about the Bible." I offered, squirming in my seat on the porch glider.

"Asking questions is never a sin," Sean replied, "And children should never be told that it is. You must keep in mind that when Sister Evangelina tells you something she is only giving her opinion and her opinion may not always be right."

Another thunderbolt, teachers may not always be right? Only giving her opinion? The world was turning, keeping up was going to be scary.

"But God, and Hell and Heaven and all that stuff, that's true right". Margaret Mary was strangely silent as these words poured out of me, almost in a panic.

"I believe God is in his heaven and that he has passed on to us a set of rules that will allow us to join him there one day. Our religious beliefs are a way of passing on these rules and in general help us to live good and worthy lives."

Margaret Mary was nodding her head as her father spoke and as she reached for my hand I began to realize that this was perhaps another subject that she knew more about than we had discussed before. As I walked home that night I realized yet another window of the real world had been opened up for me. I could not as yet see clearly through it but now I could see shades of gray from that black and white vista of my rapidly fading childhood.

"Fadda Murphy, Fadda Murphy," Peter's hand was waving like a flag. In the back of the classroom Sister Mary Evangelina leaned forward in her chair, ready to pounce. Father Murphy looked up from his text.

"What is it young man?"

"Fadda, what if there was this tribe of Eskimos who lived way up in Alaska where nobody had been before except them?" Peter was getting a head of steam up. Sister Evangelina was halfway out of her chair.

"And this tribe of Eskimos were like good guys who didn't do anything wrong ever, but they never heard about Jesus, would they all go to hell when they died?"

The good sister was on the move. Father Murphy stopped her with a wave of his hand.
"Just a moment, Sister. I want to answer the boy's question before you escort him to the land of cloaks and jackets."

Sister Evangelina stopped in her tracks, huffing and puffing. Giving
Peter a "we'll see about this later look", she returned to her seat.

"May I ask your name young man?" Father Murphy closed his book
and sat on the front edge of the teacher's desk.

"Peter, Faddah, Peter Rayburn."

Father Murphy nodded and smiled. "Well Peter, that's an interesting
question, isn't it? Can people, Eskimos or not, still go to heaven if
they lead a good life and are good people? Is that what you want to
know?"

Peter nodded his head. So did I. So did Margaret Mary.

"Let me ask you a question," Father Murphy began, "If you were in
charge of who went to heaven and who did not, would you let these
Eskimos in?"

"Yeah, I mean, Yes Faddah, if they were good and didn't have any
sins or nuthin'."

"And why would you do that?"

That one had Peter stumped for a moment. He was undoubtedly
figuring how much time in the cloak room his answer was going to
bring. "'Cause Heaven is for good people and that's where they are
supposed to go." Peter checked over his shoulder quickly to get a
locate on Sister Evangelina. "And why wouldn't you be thinking Jesus
might not feel the same way?"

"Cause it don't say so in the Bible, it says only people who believe in
Jesus get to go to heaven." Peter was sure he was right again and
ready to stand his ground. Margaret Mary even nodded her head in
agreement. I stared straight ahead, watching from the corner of my
eye and listening very carefully.

"And so, young Mr. Rayburn, what does believing in Jesus mean to
you?" Peter checked over his shoulder for Sister Evangelina before

answering. "It means like believing Jesus was a real guy and came down from heaven to save us all from our sins and got killed and stuff." There was the slightest hint of uncertainty in Peter's voice as he answered.

"And is that all it is meaning to you?" Father Murphy added.

And then an amazing thing happened, Margaret Mary's hand shot up in the air and she stood up beside her desk and added,
"Believing in Jesus also means you should be a good person and treat other people the way you want to be treated. My father told me that and I believe it."

And for the rest of my life I would wish I had raised my hand right then and said, "Me too." Instead I turned in my chair to see if Sister Evangelina was swooping down on Margaret Mary. Father Murphy smiled.

"I don't believe I have ever heard a better definition of what believing in Jesus meant young lady." And then he turned to Peter. "Do you agree with that young man?

Peter nodded his head and said, "Yes, I do Father."

"Then surely the Eskimos will go to heaven." Father Murphy concluded.

Skepticism is the beginning of faith

Oscar Wilde

Chapter 4

TWO CLAMS

"Two clams and a sinker. Send 'em back down."

That's my Dad speaking, in our twelve foot, Ted Williams Model aluminum car top fishing boat purchased right out of last year's 1958 Sears Roebuck catalog for $129. In the boat, along with my Dad, are myself, Teddy, my brother Bob and his friend Tommy, and my brother John and his friend, Mike. Close quarters for sure, but there we were, all seven of us, bobbing around in York Harbor, Maine on a summer Saturday morning, long, long ago.

All six of us kids were bottom fishing for flounder with "drop lines", home-made fishing rigs consisting of four wooden clothes pins stuck together to form a square and maybe, fifteen or twenty foot of fishing line wrapped about. Add two hooks and a lead sinker and we were ready to fish. Practically.

You see the routine went something like this: after my Dad positioned each of us kids in the tiny boat so that it did not tip over or sink, we would put out into the middle of York harbor. After dropping anchor my Dad would patiently bait each of our lines, two clams each on two staggered fish hooks. Then we would lower our rig over the side of the boat, letting out the line until the weight hit the bottom. At this point each of us would immediately assume we had a bite, tug upward frantically on our lines and begin pulling up the whole works. Usually this exercise ended with my Dad examining our empty hooks and proclaiming, in his hearty, jovial voice,

"Two clams and a sinker, send 'em back down."

And this exercise would repeat itself, every thirty seconds or so, as we bobbed about in the early morning harbor, so much more than fishing.

American David Ferrier was born on November 7, 1925 in Lowell, Massachusetts. He was the oldest boy and second child of Alvin &

Mary Ferrier, my grandparents, who had come to America from Brazil in their early twenties. They were of Portuguese descent and upon maneuvering the processes of Ellis Island, Alvin's surname, Ferreira became transposed to Ferrier and such it would remain despite a host of Ferreira aunts and uncles and cousins and the like.

Time and tide carried Alvin and Mary to Lowell where millwork and factory jobs were to be had and my grandfather found work in those mills as he raised his three children. My Dad grew up on the ball fields and parks of a section of Lowell called Wigginville and likely would have followed his father into the mills had it not been for the onset of World War II and the carnage and opportunity it offered.

My Dad enlisted in the Army Air Corps in June of 1943, one week after he graduated from high school. He would eventually be assigned as a tail gunner in B-24 Liberator Bombers attached to the Eighth Air Force Bomber Group flying out of England, where he served until the war's end.

The Eight Air Force had deployed to the European Theatre of Operations in 1942. By the time my father joined the unit they had suffered over 47,000 airmen casualties and lost over 12,000 heavy bombers to the German Luftwaffe. Seventeen members of this unit were awarded the Medal of Honor. After the war I never heard my father speak of his military service. Other than some fading sepia photographs, his memories were kept in a wooden box in the basement of our home, secretly plundered and wondered at by his three children.

Family history relates that prior to his leaving for England he first met my mother one summer weekend at the bandstand in Hampton Beach, New Hampshire. They would exchange letters during his time away and when he returned to Lowell in May of 1946 they became engaged. They were married that fall and one year and one month later I arrived, a year later my brother, Bob, and two years after that, my brother John.

By the time he was 25, my mother, 24, they had three children. My mother stayed home at first to raise us, my Dad worked two jobs to pay the bills. On my birth certificate his occupation is listed as "woodworker", and on weekends he worked in a bowling alley. We lived, during these early years, in the housing projects, low income housing which gave a preference to returning veterans.

In addition to both jobs, using his GI Bill Educational Benefits, he attended night school at Lowell Technical College for six long years, three nights a week, to obtain his Bachelor's Degree in Textile Engineering. Though I was very young I recall my Dad coming home from work around 5PM, sitting with us at dinner and then going off to catch a bus across the city to attend his night school classes. He would return long after our bedtimes but often I would wake up or lie awake till he came home. The clock near my bed would read 11PM or slightly later. Next morning he would have a quick breakfast with us and take another bus to his day job assembling cabinets in a cabinet factory. Woodworker.

Amidst all this my father found time to teach me and my brothers to tie our shoes, comb our hair, catch a baseball and ride our bikes. I recall his doing these things with patience and delight as we mastered these tasks. And though we lived in public housing, never owned a car and we brothers rotated clothing among ourselves, there was never any sense of poverty, or lack in our home. Family gatherings among aunts and uncles and cousins and grandparents were frequent and joyous, celebrating a herd of holidays, birthdays, anniversaries, graduations and Sunday dinners.

When his night schooling was finished and a better job beckoned we were able to move from the housing projects into our own home in the newly developed Belvedere section of the city. One of the first things he did when we moved to our new home was build and dedicate a shrine to Our Lady of Fatima in our side yard. Statues of Mary, three kneeling children and a lamb were nestled in a beautiful stand of white birch trees beside our home. My Dad had promised that if he ever was able to have a home for his family he would build this shrine.

His first car was a 1956 Ford station wagon, two tone blue with plenty of room for kids. My Dad would always fill that station wagon with kids, whether for a ride to the beach or a trip to a neighborhood ice cream stand. Amidst all the ups and downs, trials and tribulations of growing up I was always sure of one thing, that both my father and my mother were doing their best for us, for me, with the resources and talents and sacrifices they brought to their marriage.

While my Mom cooked meals and washed clothes and picked up after the lot of us my Dad was the organizer of weekend camping trips, backyard ball games, snowball fights and cook outs. We attended Catholic Mass every Sunday as a family and I still recall how proud he was of me when I memorized enough Latin to become an Altar Boy at our parish church. Good grades and good deeds were recognized and rewarded and this instilled in me a desire to deserve and earn their affection and love.

My Mom never accompanied us on these York Harbor fishing trips. They were strictly guy business. Even Margaret Mary, my other most constant companion, never made it aboard our Saturday morning fishing boat. She seldom came with us on our weekend trips to Maine. Not so secretly she feared leaving her father home alone with the whiskey and the sadness that made it indispensable. This was not something we ever spoke about, just understood, as children often do among themselves. And that would leave my Mom the lone female amongst the cavorting boys club that our weekends in Maine were. She bore up well, given the chaos of her surroundings and I never heard her complain of the circumstance.

Jacqueline Theresa Ferrier, nee L'Esperance, was born in Lowell, Massachusetts on April 23, 1926. She was the oldest of two children born to Walter and Mary L'Esperance, my maternal grandparents. Mary died when my mother was very young, leaving Walter with two small children to raise amidst the Great Depression. Family history relates that Walter, who served overseas with the 26th Yankee Division in World War I, faltered as a businessman, operating and losing several small storefront businesses through the thirties and forties. He eventually remarried and a third child, my Mother's half-sister and my beloved aunt, Eileen, was added to the struggling family. By all accounts my Mother's relationship with her step-mother was contentious and by seventeen my Mother had moved from her home to a room in the local YWCA where she was living when she met my father.

Sadly, my grandfather, Walter, took his own life when I was a small child as did my mother's younger brother, my Uncle Sonny, when I was in high school. Suicide, like a familial dark curtain hung over my Mother's family as a shroud and I would never know how much her frequent deep depressions later in life may have brought her to the verge of this tragic ending.

The first thing I remember about my Mother was her great physical beauty. By any yardstick she was a stunner. In her wedding dress alongside my Dad in the timeless color photographs, in scratchy, jumpy home movies carrying birthday cakes or shepherding us around playgrounds she was radiant, aglow.

But off camera, through the years, there was a sadness in my Mother, repressed anger and hurt never spoken of which festered and grew through the years. Though as children we had no inkling of the adult, husband and wife, lovers and companions issues which existed between her and my Dad, they were there, smoke in the tree line, distant thunder, some of the time. But these dark clouds tell only part of my Mother's story.

Among all my parents friends, family, neighbors and acquaintances she was the first woman to get her driver's license, an almost unheard of presumption among the domesticated housewives back in the day. And once my brothers and I were all safely started in school she got herself a job, an outside the house, paycheck producing job, another marked anomaly in that era. I recall her coming home smelling of delicious chocolate, from her first job, packing cookies into paper cups in a cookie factory. I also remember her soaking her hands in a saucer of medicine to soothe the many tiny paper cuts lacerating her fingertips.

When we moved from the housing projects to our new home in Belvedere she found work with Raytheon Electronics, a job she held for almost twenty years. None of my aunts, wonderful women who they were, ever worked outside of the home, at least not full time. They never drove either, such was not the fashion of the day in hardscrabble Lowell, Massachusetts anyway. A woman's place was in the home, taking care of her children, washing clothes, cooking meals, cleaning house, all of which she did, but she worked, hard, outside the home to contribute to our well-being, to put some more money into the pot and, I suspect, to give herself some sense of self-worth not forthcoming to the average woman in that day and age. My Mom was independent, she had a temper, and I suspect she had dreams, forever put aside for the sake of her family, a sacrifice we would never see or even imagine as the years rolled by and her sadness increased. From my Dad I learned to be a man, from my Mom I learned about sacrifice without anyone ever realizing the cost of what was lost.

"I got one Mr. Ferrier, I got one!" Tommy Carrel yanked furiously on his line and began hauling it in.

"Me too," I yelped, tugging my line upward. Within a few seconds it was obvious that Tommy had me and I him as my Dad patiently untangled our lines and got us ready to resume our imitation of fishing. Once all of our lines were back in the water my Dad would repair to the bow of the boat and lower his line over the side. Meanwhile, among us kid's boredom was settling in. Despite our yanking our lines out of the water every sixty seconds there were no fish coming aboard. Then my Dad would say, "Bobby, come here and hold my line for a minute. I have to check the motor."

My brother would make his way to the front of the boat as my Dad carefully made his way to the back. Almost instantly Bobby began yanking Dad's line in.

"I got one, I got one!" And sure enough Bob would land a flounder. The rest of us would look on in envy and wonder as my Dad removed the hook from the fish's mouth and dropped him in the bucket. Re-baiting his hooks he would lower the line over the side, Bob would return triumphantly to his original fishing position and all would be well until my Dad would say,

"David, come here and watch my line. I have to check the motor." Yeah, you guessed it, instant bite, fish in the bucket, renewed enthusiasm through the boat until each of us had landed a fish (most often while my Dad checked the motor).

By mid-morning our fishing trip complete, we would head back to our weekend home, a luxuriously cramped and crowded travel trailer seasonally parked at Camp Eaton in York Beach. Living quarters for eight, sometimes more, were made possible by our homemade plywood and canvas porch which held two single beds, a worn and weary sleeper sofa that always smelled, and felt wet and a tiny black and white TV equipped with rabbit ears antenna, aluminum foil extensions and three channels of snowy, mostly local programming. I recall a rickety card table, lots of board games, cribbage tournaments and happiness as completing the almost outdoor décor. Inside my Mom would prepare group meals on a tiny, two burner propane stove. I remember lots of soup, Campbell's Chicken Noodle being a mainstay, along with bologna sandwiches, pots of spaghetti, and on Saturday Mornings, after the fishing trip, stacks of pancakes, gallons of milk and happy laughter.

"You shoulda' seen it Mom, everybody caught a fish except Dad!" One of us would happily announce.

"Teddy caught the biggest one, but I caught two!" And the bidding and bragging would go on around the table.

And he would smile and she would know.

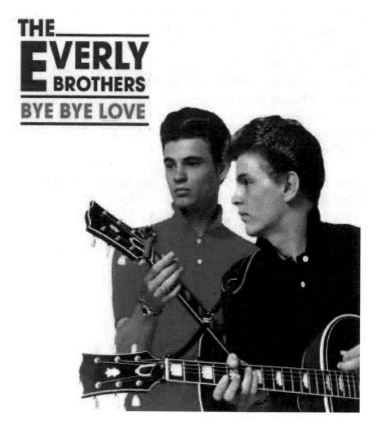

Chapter 5

DON & PHIL & THE BITTER PILL

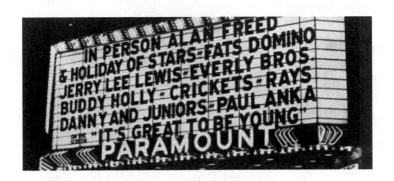

Bye Bye Love,
Bye Bye Happiness,
Hello Loneliness,
I think I'm gonna cry
Bye Bye Love,
Bye Bye Sweet Caress,
Hello Loneliness
I feel like I could die???[1]

There it was, a not so happy message sweetened by the heavenly harmonies of the Everly Brothers, Don and Phil, and reinforced by virtually every other rock and roll singer crooning from our almost teenage transistor radios.

Don't believe me? Try this one,

Well since my baby left me,
I've found a new place to dwell,
Down at the end of lonely street At Heartbreak Hotel.

---

[1] Felice & Boudleaux Bryant, Bye Bye Love

Where I get so lonely baby,
Well I'm so lonely,
I get so lonely I could die???[2]

Elvis. The King, and just one more, (of many),

Just sweet sixteen, and now you're gone
They've taken you away
I'll never kiss your lips again
They buried you today

Teen angel, can you hear me?
Teen angel, can you see me?
Are you somewhere up above?
And I am still your own true love?
Teen angel, teen angel, answer me, please.

That one is "Teen Angel" by Mark Dinning, a moving tale of how his
girlfriend gets run over by a train. You can't make this stuff up. All
three of these songs were Number One hit records, they sold millions
of copies, to kids. Lots of cryin', lots of dyin'. This love stuff was
starting to sound pretty scary. And there was lots more to come.

Rock & Roll was born, some say, somewhere between Bill Haley and
His Comets singing "Rock Around The Clock" and Chuck Berry, Fats
Domino and Little Richard wailing "race music" into the American
mainstream. Whatever the genesis, rock & roll was our music, music
written for, aimed at and performed by teenagers, for teenagers and
teenage wannabe's like me and my buddies in the far away year of
1959.

At this point Elvis had been around for three plus years, there was lots
of music that was "Be Bop A Lu La" and "Whole Lotta Shakin'
Going On" but throughout the sound stream was this troublesome aura
of impending, inevitable, unforeseeable heartbreak. I don't know
what part of my brain core was storing this sad information but it was
no doubt being packed away somewhere for future consideration.
Meanwhile we had "You Ain't Nuthin' But A Hound Dog", "Be Bop

---

[2] Elvis Presley, Mae Axton, Thomas Durden, Heartbreak Hotel

A Lu La" and other wonderful anthems to annoy our parents. Long live Rock & roll.

"She isn't my girlfriend!

I was yelling because Richie Burke was right up in my face and he had already pushed me once so I figured we were about to have a fight.

"Oh yeah, then how come you're always hanging around with her and walking home from school with her and stuff?" Richie maintained his belligerence, I was trying to maintain my cool.

"Because she's my friend, friend. Not my girlfriend, I don't even have a girlfriend!"

Then he punched me. Then I punched him back. Next we grabbed hold of each other and started rolling around on the ground. I still didn't know why we were fighting but I figured I could sort that out later. The rolling around continued for a few more minutes until Teddy and Peter and some of the other guys pulled us apart. Teddy told Ritchie he better get outta here and Ritchie turned and walked away. I was dusting myself off and trying to figure out what had happened.

"Wow!" Teddy exclaimed, "You got a shiner!"

"I do?" Feeling my face I got to the sore spot under my eye.

"That's okay though" Peter added, checking out my eye, "Ritchie got a bloody nose. You tagged him pretty good."

"I did?" The details were a little hazy.

"Not as good as when Butchie beat him up, but not bad." Teddy added.

"That guy better learn to fight better if he's gonna keep getting in fights." Peter decided as my breathing returned to normal and my hands stopped shaking.

"What were we fighting about anyway? How come he got so mad?"

"I think he likes Margaret Mary. He's always asking me about her."
Steve Gagnon said. Steve was another one of my Shedd Park buddies
who went to school with us at the Immaculate.

"And because of that he picks a fight with me?"

"There's a reason that guy keeps getting beat up." Teddy offered as I
dusted myself off and wondered how I was going to explain my black
eye to my parents. And to Margaret Mary.

Love Hurts, Love Scars.
Love Wounds and Mars,
Any heart no tough,
Or strong enough,
To take a lot of pain, take a lot of pain,
Love is like a cloud, holds a lot of rain, Love hurts,
Ooh, love hurts.[3]

"What happened to your eye?" Margaret Mary exclaimed when I
went over to her house that night.

I had already been through the story with my Mom and Dad but with
Margaret Mary, as usual, I was looking more for answers than just
repeating the explanation.

"Richie Burke socked me in the eye because I told him I wasn't your
boyfriend!"

It took a lot to stump Margaret Mary but I could tell right then she was
stumped, big time stumped.

"Start at the beginning," she said as she led me onto her front porch,
"Tell me everything."

---

[3] Boudleaux Bryant, Love Hurts.

So I did. I told her what happened but without a clue as to why. Then I told her what Steve Gagnon said about how Richie Burke liked her and was always asking about her and stuff.

"And because of that he beats you up?"

"He didn't beat me up! We beat each other up. He got a bloody nose."

"And you got a black eye and that makes sense?"

"Not to me, I was kinda' hoping you could figure it out though."

Margaret Mary folded her hands in her lap, gathered her thoughts and took a deep breath.

"First of all I don't even know Richie Burke."

"Yes you do, he's the guy Butchie Martin beat up for looking at his sister". I added helpfully.

"That's not what I mean. Listen to me, just because somebody says they like you doesn't mean you have to be their boyfriend or girlfriend. You understand?

"Yes", (of course not). I was on new ground here.
"I've never met Richie Burke and if he's the type of person that's always getting into fights I don't ever want to."

"Okay, I get that", I actually did, "but why did he want to pick a fight with me?"

"I don't know. That's what you and I are going to ask him after school tomorrow."

"I'm not doing that! I just had a fight with the guy!"

"Yes, you are."

"But why?"

"Because I am asking you to and if you asked me to do something like this, I would."

I still didn't want to go see Richie Burke but now I felt like I had to, or should, and would because I figured if Margaret Mary thought it was the right thing to do I should do it. Slowly but surely I was learning.

So we did. We met up with Richie Burke at Shedd Park the next afternoon and the first thing he said was that he didn't want to fight anymore. I said neither did I, but I was still kind of ticked off that he picked a fight with me.

Richie was acting real nervous because Margaret Mary was there and she didn't say anything until we got the fighting thing out of the way. When she spoke it was with her softest, kindest voice,

"I'm glad you two have made up." Then she stepped forwarded and held her hand out to Ritchie. "I'm Margaret Mary Sullivan, I'm glad to meet you."

And Ritchie stood there, staring at the ground and turning red as a beat. He didn't shake Margaret Mary's hand, just shuffled his feet in the dirt. Margaret Mary lowered her hand and said, "Richie, why did you pick a fight with David about me?"

First I thought Richie was going to run away, which is something I probably would have done, but finally he mumbled, "I don't know."

"Yes you do", Margaret Mary answered, "And I want to know why, please."

Richie actually managed to turn a redder red than beet red and finally looked Mary Margaret in the eye.

"I guess it was because I thought he was your boyfriend."

"Why would you want to beat him up because he was my boyfriend?" Margaret Mary asked, again in a gentle, questioning way.

"I don't know." Ritchie went back to his staring at his shuffling feet posture. I was staying way out of this one.

"Yes you do, Ritchie. We all know why we do things, only sometimes we get embarrassed someone will laugh at us if we say why."

I figured nodding my head about now was the right gesture and I caught Richie's eye with a look that said, "Boy, am I glad I'm not you right now." And suddenly I wasn't ticked off at Richie anymore.

Finally Richie answered, "I guess because I want to be your boyfriend and I was mad at him because he is."

"David is not my boyfriend and you are not going to be my boyfriend. Right now nobody is going to be my boyfriend. I've got lots of other things to do besides be somebody's girlfriend."

This was another one of those situations where you could practically see the steam coming out of Margaret Mary's ears. But when Margaret Mary said this all the tension seemed to go out of the air. This was no longer about me over Ritchie, or who Margaret Mary liked best. This was about Margaret Mary being herself, first and foremost, a lesson both Ritchie and I had yet to learn. He meanwhile was looking totally miserable so I chimed in, hoping to make him feel better,

"Yeah, and besides, I don't even want Margaret Mary to be my girlfriend."

I had just embarked upon a lifelong habit of knowing when to say exactly the wrong thing at exactly the right time. But if you could have seen the look of bemused tolerance on Margaret Mary's face when I said this you would know why I have forever held her in my heart.

After Richie left and Margaret Mary and I were walking home I asked, "So, we're still friends right?"

Margaret Mary smiled and took my hand.

"You are my friend because I like you and think you are smart, when you let yourself be, which you are getting better at, sometime." I nodded, pretty sure that was a compliment.

"But I'm not your boyfriend?" I was teasing, a little.

"No, not yet anyway, maybe even not later. But you are my very best, most important friend, and that, I think, is more important than being my boyfriend."

I nodded and smiled and for the very first, but not the last time, I wished in my heart that Margaret Mary was my girlfriend.

I've been made blue,
I've been lied to,
When will I be loved?[4]

More words of wisdom from the Everly Brothers. I could hardly wait.

---

[4] When will I be Loved, Phil Everly.

Music gives a soul to the universe, wings to the mind, flight to the imagination, and life to everything

Plato, 460 B.C.

Kennedy Nixon debate, Sept. 26, 1960

Chapter 6

THE GREAT DEBATE

"That guy looks like a crook to me."

Teddy Gianoulous speaking, as he, along with Margaret Mary, her father, Sean, my father and I gathered around our 18 inch, black and white only television set to watch the first televised debate between Presidential candidates Richard Milhous Nixon and John Fitzgerald Kennedy on the night of September 26, 1960.

My Mom would come in and out of the living room throughout the debate as she ironed school clothes and cleaned around the house. My brothers were in the back room pouting because they couldn't watch Zorro.

"And doesn't young Mr. Kennedy appear to be a broth of a lad?" Sean commented as he sipped on a bottle of Guinness Stout.

And indeed candidate Kennedy looked tanned, trim, rested and ready next to a haggard and perspiring Richard Nixon as the debate progressed.

"My brother Chris said that Kennedy guy was like a hero in the war. He drove PT boats and crashed one and got lots of medals." Teddy pitched in.

"He wrote a book about it called "PT 109". I did a book report on it." I added.

"He didn't write a book, John Hersey wrote a story about him. That must have been quite a book report." Margaret Mary chided.

"That's what I meant, I put it in my book report. I got an A plus."

"So did I," Teddy offered, of course he should have, he copied my book report.

"I wonder if that other guy was in the war." I asked.

"Navy," my Dad said, "Some kind of clerk or something, but he was there."

"Yeah, but he didn't crash a boat and get a lot of medals like our guy." Teddy concluded.

Our guy. The local propaganda machine was working well.

"Mr. Ferrier, as a veteran yourself are you of the opinion that military service should be a prerequisite for holding high office?" Sean asked.

"Well, it certainly didn't hurt Ike any, or Truman before him, but we have had some fine leaders who never served in the military."

"Franklin Delano Roosevelt, our thirty second president, did not serve in the military." Margaret Mary chimed in.

"Neither did Abraham Lincoln," I added. I had just completed a book report on Abraham Lincoln. That got me a smile from Margaret Mary.

"Hard to say a bad word about those two," my father said, "So I would say Sean, military service is a plus, no question, but doesn't have to be a prerequisite."

"Growing up in Belfast as I did, we were not so fond of the soldiers in our parishes."

"Soldiers often draw unpopular duty", my Dad responded, "Doesn't necessarily mean they are bad soldiers."

"And in Belfast the conflict continues." Sean finished his stout and shook his head sadly.

Meanwhile Margaret Mary and I sat cross legged on the floor with our school notebooks in our laps taking notes. While these first ever televised debates between presidential candidates may have been a groundbreaking first for the American public, for us they were homework, assigned by the quasi-benevolent Sister Mary of Charity, our eighth grade teacher.

"I want you each to write a paper on why our own Catholic Senator, from right here in Massachusetts among us, should become the next President of the United States." The good Sister commanded, "And I want you all to watch the television tonight while our own John Fitzgerald Kennedy puts that heathen Republican in his place."

No ambiguity there. Opposing views were not welcome, or wise. Even Peter Rayburn wouldn't bite on that one.

So we watched and learned that both candidates thought that Communism was bad, America was good and that we had the finest form of government in the world. Margaret Mary was scribbling madly in her notebook. I was empty after Communism bad, America good.

As the broadcast went on John Kennedy always looked directly into the camera when commenting, relaxed and confident.

Nixon, on the other hand, shifted his gaze, sometimes looking to the assembled reporters on the sides of the stage when answering, other times referring to his written notes with downward glances. He was polishing the "Tricky Dick" image without even knowing it.

As you may have already guessed, Richard Nixon had no fans in our living room that night and scarce few throughout New England. He had served a rather undistinguished eight years as Vice President under Dwight Eisenhower and done little to endear himself to the people of New England, or even Dwight Eisenhower for that matter. Nevertheless he was the front running Republican candidate and despite his regional drawbacks and disheveled appearance was giving young Prince Kennedy all he could handle in the current campaign.

John Kennedy on the other hand was to regional royalty born. He had, to this point, served admirably in the Senate, casting a celebrity glamor about himself as he regaled and charmed the media, particularly the burgeoning monster called television. He looked good, sounded good, dressed well and was movie star perfect when the cameras were on. He had an elegant, photogenic wife and baby daughter, mountains of family money and prestige to drive his campaign and the full weight and support of the Democratic machine behind him.

But he also had a grievous, un-disputable, inescapable flaw of character hounding him throughout his campaign. He was a Catholic. Never before had a candidate for the presidency embraced this religious persuasion and rampant rumors that his election would mean his elected office would always be clandestinely subservient to the Pope in Rome screamed from the tabloid and not so tabloid headlines. What was a blessing in predominantly Irish Beantown hounded him, particularly in the southern states and throughout the Midwest.

Richard Nixon however was a Quaker, or some kind of lapsed, nondescript Protestant Caucasian, unblemished by the Holy See in Rome. Nixon was old school Republican politics, safe as could be, right down the middle, with just the right slant of right wing rhetoric. What worked against him was an undeniable, fundamental lack of charisma or charm. He was a gray suit with a drab tie sweating through his pancake makeup under the unforgiving lens of the network cameras.

In a comment picked up by the national media by Mayor Richard Daley of Chicago, in whose city the debates were taking place, was quoted as saying while watching Nixon on camera, "My God, they've embalmed him and he isn't even dead." That type of perception wouldn't woo a lot of voters.

'Sean, can I bring you another beer?" My Mom asked from the kitchen doorway.

"A pint would do nicely, thank you Mrs. Ferrier."

"Jackie will do fine Sean", my Mom replied, "Mrs. Ferrier sounds like Dave's mother is in the house." And she shuddered a secret shudder as she turned back into the kitchen.

Margaret Mary put down her notebook and followed.

"Thank you for having us over tonight," she said as my Mom handed her a cold bottle of Stout from the refrigerator. There was no TV in Margaret Mary's house, never would be in all the time we were growing up.

"Cursed things bring nothing but confusion to the household," Sean had announced when I asked him why there was no TV.

"If I want to watch TV I can always come over to your house, can't I," Margaret Mary added, and as I nodded my head she said, "Well that's even better than having my own TV, isn't it."

"Hey! It's coming back on again, you better hurry up." I yelled from the living room after we had been properly commercialized to buy laundry soap, toilet paper and a Ford Falcon automobile.

But Margaret Mary was not done in the kitchen with my Mom. Still holding the bottle of stout, she whispered, "Mrs. Ferrier, does Mr. Ferrier ever drink too much and you wish he wouldn't?"

My Mom took Margaret Mary over to the kitchen table where they sat down next to each other. Keeping her voice low my Mom answered, "No dear, he does not. But my father did, and often, and that did not end well."

"Is there anything you can do about it?" Margaret Mary pleaded.

"Not that I know of, you can plead or beg or try to reason with them but if they are going to drink too much, they are going to drink too much."

"Then come see me when you feel sad. Sad is something I know a little bit about." My Mom squeezed Margaret Mary's hand to seal their secret pact.

Margaret Mary hurried back to the living room, handing her father his beer knowing unhappily, that this one wasn't too much, but that it wasn't enough either.

"Did I miss anything good?" Margaret Mary directed her question at me. I was still back on Communism bad, American good. Before I could answer Sean took a grateful sip of his beverage and said,

"Candidate Kennedy is clearly winning the likeability contest but neither of them has shocked the world with his rhetoric as yet."

"Looking good is not going to be enough to get him elected," my Dad said, "but it's not going to hurt him either."

I wrote that down without wondering how Sister Mary of Charity was going to like that remark.

And so the rest of the event passed, civilly, each man silent and respectful as the other spoke, neither disagreeing sharply on any of the major issues, but overall Candidate Kennedy clearly came away with the upper hand. John Kennedy would go on to win the presidency that year by the smallest margin in American history, winning the popular vote by two tenths of one percent, the closest margin of the twentieth century. Subsequent years would throw doubt as to how these votes were tallied, what back room deals may have affected the outcome, but on that night, the promise of Camelot was born, launched and sustained by a more photogenic candidate outshining an old school warhorse.

Tragically, both of these men would go on to win the presidency in years to come. Neither would complete his term in office. Both would leave under tragic circumstance and would not be judged kindly by history.

"That guy looks like a crook to me."

Nostradamus had nothing on my buddy, Teddy Gianoulous.

"In the election of 1860, Abraham Lincoln said the question was whether this nation could exist half-slave and half-free. In the election of 1960, and with the world around us, the question is whether the WORLD will exist half-slave and half-free, whether it will move in the direction of freedom, in the direction of the road we are taking, or whether it will move in the direction of slavery."

**From John Kennedy's opening statement
in the first Kennedy-Nixon debate.**

"Um, the things that Senator Kennedy said, um, many of us can agree with."

**From Richard Nixon's opening statement,
same night, same debate.**

"That son of a bitch just lost us the election."

**Reported remarks of Nixon's running mate, Henry
Cabot Lodge, following the first debate.**

Chapter 7

ALL THE STARS THAT TWINKLE IN THE SKY

My birthday is on the 12th of December, smack dab in the middle of Christmas shopping prime time. My Brother Bob's birthday is December 18th and my cousin Dick's is on December 8th. We are a close family and all three of our birthdays would generally be lumped into one large and happy three cake party. Birthdays of course, mean presents, and birthday presents in mid-December are leavened by the impending receipt of presents, Christmas types, coming in two very long and much anticipated weeks. This usually results in another plaid shirt for school, or a hopefully un-funky sweater to wear over the old plaid shirt. But the cakes were delicious, the parties fun and the family gatherings joyous.

However the focus here, the jumping off point for this particular tale, is the presents. Up until now, the occasion of my twelfth birthday, presents were always something I received, gifts I had coming, a one-way street of getting, gratefully, what was coming to me by birth or circumstance. All that was about to change and, not surprisingly, Margaret Mary was the bringer of change in her wonderful, as always, fashion.

"It's for you, for your birthday." Margaret Mary held the small, beautifully wrapped package out to me. "You can open it now if you want."

I wanted, but I hesitated. I know this will sound odd, but up until then birthday presents had always been family affairs. When there was a party usually it was at my Uncle Dick and Aunt Kay's house, filled with cousins and brothers, aunts and uncles, Moms and Dads and grandparents. School friends and the gang from Shedd Park were generally not there, my Uncle Dick lived across town and like I said, the parties were generally family affairs. Yet here was Margaret Mary holding out a gift for me. Very special. A bit unsettling. More new ground.

I took the package, small, way too small for a shirt, wrapped in gold paper with a green bow. There was also a card, there's always a card.

"Thank you," was all I could stammer. I was genuinely moved, a bit confused by the gesture, grateful but uneasy.

"It's from my father and me, but I picked it out. Go ahead, open it."

So I did. In a beautiful wooden case, which flipped open lengthwise, was a handsome green and gold Parker fountain pen set, the first I had ever seen outside of a store window. The pen had a gold plated nib, was fat as a gambler's cigar, with a tiny gold lever to draw ink into the rubber bladder within the pen's tube. Alongside this treasure, slim and gorgeous as well, was a mechanical pencil, perfectly matched to the pen. I was flabbergasted, I couldn't think of what to say. Margaret Mary was standing there smiling, waiting for me to say something.

"This is really neat," I managed to stammer, "Really, I like it a lot. Thank you." And in return I got that one of a kind, best in the world smile from Margaret Mary. "Well, I'm glad you like it. You will have to write very special things with these, that's why we got them for you."

Dazzled by the pen set I almost completely forgot about the card but the look on Margaret Mary's face reminded me and I set my gift aside and opened the card. A baseball player grinned at me from the cover, "Happy Birthday" inscribed on the scoreboard over his shoulder. I opened the card and read,

"The two most important days in your life are the day you were born and the day you find out why." Samuel Clemens.

My favorite writer, favorite person I'd never know, secret guy I'd really like to be. Only Margaret Mary knew that. Under that another quote,

"The world is full of magic things waiting for our senses to grow sharper." William Butler Yeats.

From Sean's favorite writer, his Mark Twain.

Then signed, "Happiest of Birthdays, MM & Sean."

Now I really didn't know what to say. Suddenly there was a lump in my throat and my eyes were filled with tears. What the hell? Then Margaret Mary hugged me and my confusion meter went right off the scale.

That night I proudly showed my pen set to my Mom and Dad. "How very nice," my Mom said.

"Pretty special," said my Dad. "You'll have to wait for Saturday to get your gift from us. We're all going over to Kay and Dick's for a party."

Plaid shirt here I come.

"Could I ask Margaret Mary if she wants to come? And maybe Teddy?" I found myself saying. I had never had my friends at a family party before and I think perhaps I was starting to realize that my personal family was beginning to include people I was not related to.

"Of course," my Mom replied. "If it's alright with their parents it's alright with us."

But Margaret Mary was going on the train into Boston with her father on Saturday and Teddy was going to work with his Dad at the garage. The union of my two tribes would have to wait for another occasion.

So on Saturday, amidst a house full of family, I watched my cousin Dick unwrap his blue, red and green checkered shirt, then in my turn I unveiled my green, red and blue checkered shirt. There was very little suspense when my brother Bob revealed his shirt of three familiar colors. But the birthday cakes were great, with ice cream aplenty, wax cups of sugary tonic, the Lowell name for soda, and gleeful anticipation of not far off Christmas presents to come.

Twelve years old was a big deal for me, the brink of adolescence, not yet a teenager but certainly not a little kid any more either. I had already outgrown Santa Claus, short pants, afternoon naps and babysitters. Last summer had been my last in Little League, onward to Babe Ruth League in the coming spring, grade school graduation in June and gasp, High School in the fall. But first of all there was Christmas and for the first time in my life I decided I was going Christmas shopping, for them, my family and my friends.

"This one is neat, it's got a fish on it!" Teddy was waving a baseball hat at me from across the store. It was yellow with a blue fish on the front. Just what I wanted for my Dad.

"How much is it?" I asked.

Teddy checked the tag. "Three dollars."

"Okay, I've got three dollars. What size is it?"

"I don't know," Teddy checked inside, "It says seven and half. What size does your Dad wear?"

"I don't know, put it on, maybe we can tell from that."

Teddy pulled the hat on. It came down over his ears, appropriately big. Earlier I had bought my Mother a bottle of White Shoulders perfume. It cost four dollars. I still had twelve dollars left from my snow shoveling money. I got each of my brothers a giant comic book, the Christmas issues, Donald Duck for John, he was still a little kid, and Superman for Bob. I still liked Superman, so did Bob.

Walking home with Teddy, and my gifts, I felt good, pleased with what I had purchased and anxious to give them to my family. I still had two more gifts to buy but I couldn't get them with Teddy. One was a record album for Teddy, "Have Twangy Guitar Will Travel" by Duane Eddy. Teddy loved Duane Eddy and said he wanted to learn to play the guitar just like him. I didn't have enough money to buy Teddy a guitar so I figured a record was the next best thing.

The last one was for Margaret Mary, of course. I had no idea what to get her so I asked my Mom and she said a hairbrush and comb set would be nice and that she would help me pick one out if I wanted. So down city we went, Mom and me, and found the best brush and comb set I ever saw and when it was three dollars more than I had left my Mom paid the extra and had the store wrap it in Christmas paper and my first ever Christmas shopping experience was complete.

Come Christmas morning our tree was draped in tinsel and flickering with colored lights, with mounds and stacks of brightly wrapped gifts piled beneath and three pajama clad brothers ready to dive into the hoard. Yet with all that before me I couldn't wait to go get the gifts I had bought for my family from under my bed and pass them out.

So Dad got his hat, which he didn't take off for the whole rest of the day, Mom hugged me and said the perfume was perfect, her absolute favorite, and both my brothers looked at their comics with happiness in their eyes. This Christmas, for the first time, I appreciated all the gifts I had received but felt the absolute best about those I had given.

"It's for you, for Christmas." This time it was Margaret Mary who was a bit unsettled staring at the brightly wrapped package I was holding. And there was, of course, a card.

Earlier that evening, after our turkey had been eaten, our Christmas pies and cookies devoured I went over to Teddy's house to give him his gift. Connie answered the door and told me Teddy was in bed, he wasn't feeling good. I saw Chris sitting at the kitchen table having coffee. They had a small Christmas tree in their living room with presents they hadn't opened yet. It didn't look very Christmassy in there to me.

"I can come back later, or tomorrow or something if you want." I offered.

"No, come on in, maybe you can cheer him up a little." Connie let me in and when I walked past Chris he kind of said hello to me while he lit up a cigarette. Teddy sat up in bed when I came in and I could tell he was surprised to see me.

"I brought you something for Christmas." I said holding the present out in front of me.

"Wow", Teddy said, eyeing the package, "but I didn't get you nuthin'."

"That's okay, Teddy, I didn't get this so you would have to get something for me."

I handed Teddy his gift and the paper was off in a flash. I wish you could have seen his face when he saw the album.

"Wow!" he said, much louder than the first time, "this is so great." Teddy was out of bed in an instant.

"Connie! Look what I got!" Connie was in the kitchen with Chris when Teddy came roaring in, waving his present. "Can I use your record player? Can I? Can I play my record on it?"

"Of course", Connie said.

Chris held his hand out to Teddy. "Lemme see that." Teddy handed Chris the record and Chris turned it over and checked both sides.

"Cool gift", he announced. "C'mon I'll listen to it with you." Teddy was beaming as he followed Chris to the front room.

"You comin?" He asked as they went.

"No, I got to get going. I'll listen to it with you tomorrow though." Connie was smiling when she let me out the kitchen door and as I walked away I thought it felt a lot more like Christmas in there now.

So now Margaret Mary was holding her brush and comb and there was a silence in the room.

"Tortoise shell, My Mom said. I guess that means it's made out of a turtle."

"It's beautiful," Margaret Mary said in a choked voice. "But you didn't have to."

"I didn't get it because I had to, I got it because I wanted to. Now open the card."

Putting her gift aside Margaret Mary opened the red envelope that held the card I had picked out. It had a manger and a star, camels and baby Jesus in the middle. Inside it said "Happy Holidays", but under that I had written,

"You make every day feel like Christmas to me. Thank You for being my friend."

Margaret Mary started to say something, then spun around and ran out of the room, clutching her brush and comb, and the card. I just sort of stood there not knowing what to do and finally decided I should go home. Then Sean came into the room.

"It seems my daughter liked her gift."

"She's not mad at me is she?" Was the brightest question I could think of asking.

"Mad is not the word I would use, no."

Sean was smiling as he said this and then Margaret Mary came back into the room. She stood right in front of me and took my hand.

"Thank you for my gift. I love it. But most of all I loved what you wrote in my card."

Then she kissed me on the cheek.

I was stunned, it felt like my face was on fire. I think I stammered something about having to go home and "I'll see you tomorrow", as I backed out of their living room.

As I walked along the snow shoveled sidewalk in the chill Christmas evening a precious thought occurred to me. I had discovered two very special things this Christmas, the absolute joy of giving gifts to my family and friends and that I was indeed capable of writing very special things with my new pen set.

THE INAUGURAL ADDRESS OF

John Fitzgerald Kennedy

PRESIDENT OF THE UNITED STATES

WASHINGTON, D.C.   JANUARY 20, 1961

Chapter 8

HATLESS, COATLESS, IN THE BRIGHT SUNSHINE

"Let the word go forth from this time and place, to friend and foe alike, that the torch has been passed to a new generation of Americans – born in this century, tempered by war, disciplined by a hard and bitter peace, proud of our ancient heritage – and unwilling to witness or permit the slow undoing of those human rights to which this nation has always been committed, and to which we are committed today at home and around the world."

We were gathered once more in our living room, listening, no entranced, by John Fitzgerald Kennedy's Inauguration Speech being rebroadcast on the CBS evening news from a snowy Friday afternoon ceremony on January 20, 1961.

Gathered around the TV were my Mom and Dad, Margaret Mary and Sean, both my brothers and Teddy, witnessing much more than an inauguration, it was more like a coronation, at least in my house and all around New England.

"Let every nation know, whether it wishes us well or ill, that we will pay any price, bear any burden, meet any hardship, support any friend, oppose any foe, in order to assure the survival and success of liberty. This we pledge – and more."

No homework assignment here, this was more of a celebration, a birth of hope for a better future, to be conducted by our own John Fitzgerald Kennedy, triumphant on the Capital steps in Washington, D.C.

"He must be cold, not wearing a jacket or nuthin'." Teddy observed.

"He doesn't look cold, he looks wonderful." A more than slightly star struck Margaret Mary replied.

"He still should have a coat on, he'll catch cold." Mom, checking in.

Yet there he was, resplendent in tux and tails, hair tossed in the winter wind, handsome and graceful, speaking with force and conviction, promising a better future, promising an evolution for our nation and our world.

"The man has a fire within to keep warm. This is a great day." Sean spoke with deep emotion, sipping a glass of Tullamore Dew as the ceremony proceeded.

"Look! There's that Nixon guy! What's he doing there?" Teddy wanted to know.

"He's the Vice President Ted, or at least he used to be. He has to be there." I added.

"He's wearing a coat. I bet he's not cold." Teddy was all over the coat thing.

"Ike's there too," My Dad said. "I voted for Mr. Kennedy but I always liked Ike."

And there they were on the Capital Portico in this chill winter day, the oldest and youngest seated Presidents, visually, verbally, emotionally passing the torch. The entire event was drenched in significance, portent of wonderful things to come, dignified, steeped in a Grace not lost on those in our gathering.

"Do you think he'll be a good President, Mr. Ferrier?" Margaret Mary asked.

"I hope so," my Dad replied, "He's made a lot of promises and I believe he'll try to keep them."

"Of course he'll keep them," Margaret Mary stated, "Why wouldn't he?"

"The world, alas, can sometimes be very harsh to the makers of promises." Sean added, sipping his whiskey.

"I believe he will too," My Mom added. "There's a sincerity about the man that I like."

"I bet those Rushin Communist guys are shakin' in their boots now." Teddy offered.

"He talked a lot more about not having a war than having one." Margaret Mary said.

"Never fearing to negotiate," Sean added, "A fine turn of the word."

"My brother Chris says if the Commies attack us again he's gonna join the Marines." Proudly, from Teddy.

"I don't think the Communists have attacked us yet, Teddy." Margaret Mary offered.

"There was Korea," my Dad said. "Somehow I don't think that one is over yet."

"Somewhere, sometime, at some disputed barricade," Sean offered, "The fighting never seems to end does it not?" Resulting in a prolonged sip of his drink.

"I hope to God we've seen enough war in our lifetime," my Mom added, "We don't need to have any more of our children gone to soldiers."

And I failed to see the worried glance she gave me and my brothers, Teddy as well.

"I think a man that's seen as much war as he has is very unlikely to get us involved in another war if he can help it." My Dad offered.

"Your lips to God's ears." Sean raised his glass in a toast.

The broadcast finished, the evening ended with a whole new sense of purpose and personal involvement instilled in us by our now new President's speech.

As he rose to leave Sean once again raised his glass and said to the room, "All changed, changed utterly, a terrible beauty is born." Then he drained his glass, placed it on the side table and he and Margaret Mary started home. When she reached our front door Margaret Mary turned and said, "That was Yeats, my Father's favorite."

She turned to leave and Teddy followed. Bedtime beckoned, tomorrow was Saturday and winter sleds were to be sledded, snowballs to be tossed, snowmen to be built. Great events must be measured against those we experience daily.

As my Mom clicked off the light in my bedroom that night I thought of what the President had said and promised myself I would try in whatever way I could to be part of his vision in the years to come. Surely twelve years old was old enough to pitch in, to get involved. I was sure of one thing, if I couldn't think of a way, I could always ask Margaret Mary and she could. I lay down with these words echoing in my head,

> *"And so, my fellow Americans, ask not what your country can do for you, ask what you can do for your country."*

> *"My fellow citizens of the world: Ask not what America will do for you, but what together we can do for the freedom of man."*

And I dreamed that I did ask, as the world asked, and I was answered everything was going to be just fine.

John F. Kennedy Inauguration, Jan. 20, 1961

Chapter 9

TWISTING WITHOUT SHOUTING

"You're gonna teach me to what?" I couldn't believe my ears.
"I am going to teach you to dance. I have been practicing with my father but dancing with your father is pathetic, so I am going to teach you so I can practice with you."

"Why?" I was missing something here. Dancing was for older kids, my parents danced. I didn't see the point. Margaret Mary usually (always) made sense, but somehow the reasoning here escaped me.

"But I don't want to learn how to dance." Brilliant statement by me.

"Of course you do. We have our graduation dance in three weeks. Don't you think it would be nice if you actually knew how to dance when you got there?"

This I hadn't given much thought. We were about to finish eighth grade, there was going to be a ceremony, with caps and gowns and diplomas, and a dance. I hadn't planned on a dance. More new ground.

"Dancing is fun, you'll like it when you know how. Please do this for me."

That was it, debate over. All I needed now was instructions, and then I had an idea.

"Can I bring Teddy?"

"Of course you can, that's a very good idea. Saturday afternoon at my house, one o'clock. Bring Teddy."

Surprisingly, Teddy was all for the idea. As we walked to Margaret Mary's house on Saturday Teddy was carrying a pink flip top box of 45 RPM records and his Duane Eddy album.

"Connie said we could borrow some of her records. There's some good ones in here, she's a real good dancer."

Teddy was happy, excited at what we were about to embark on. I was nervous, anxious. I didn't like trying something new if I didn't know whether I'd be any good at it, except for sports, I knew I was good at those.

When we got to Margaret Mary's house we were surprised to see Linda Rogers there. She was a classmate of ours from the Immaculate and a friend of Margaret Mary's. Linda looked very pretty, like she had dressed up for the occasion, so did Margaret Mary. Teddy and I were dressed for nine innings of baseball. Neither Margaret Mary nor Linda mentioned this as we came into the living room.

"Linda brought her record player and we've got some really good records to dance to," Margaret Mary announced as Teddy and I shuffled our feet and looked nervous.

"I brought some records too," Teddy added, "They're my sister's, but she said we could play them as much as we want."

"Can I see?" Linda asked as Teddy offered her the pink record box.

While Linda and Teddy sorted through the records Margaret Mary came over to me and said, "You look so nervous, this is going to be fun. I promise. Just try to relax."

Trying to relax in unfamiliar situations always made me less relaxed. I managed to nod an okay as Margaret Mary went to the record player.

"We'll start with an easy one," Margaret Mary placed Sam Cooke's, "You Send Me" on the turntable, a beautiful record, smooth as silk, and I suppose, relaxing.

Margaret Mary led me to the middle of the room as Linda did to Teddy. As the music played Margaret Mary began, "Take my hand like this," Margaret Mary guided me into the dance start position, "then place your hand on my hip, here." Hot flashes I was getting.

"Now move your feet slowly and follow me, then I'm going to follow you."

So far, so good. Linda and Teddy started to glide around the living room. Teddy was making it look easy. I was having trouble getting my feet to move.

"Okay, are you ready to try the Twist?" Linda announced as she plopped Chubby Checker's record onto the turntable. As the music started I was dumbfounded. Margaret Mary actually began twisting, Linda and Teddy were dancing all over the room, twisting their lives away. I stood frozen.

"Just do what I'm doing," Margaret Mary coaxed, "move your front leg like this and turn your arms to the music. I started slowly, feeling like a complete idiot, this was not fun. I became more self-conscious, felt more awkward and stopped, before the record stopped, stopped.

"Is something wrong?" Margaret Mary asked.

"It just feels stupid to me." Best I could do.

"It's supposed to be fun," she replied, "But if you feel stupid we can stop."

Meanwhile Teddy and Linda were twisting up a storm. I was really envious of how easily Teddy was picking up the process. The record ended. I couldn't have been more relieved.

"Let's do another!" Teddy exclaimed reaching into Connie's record box. He pulled out the "Peppermint Twist" by Joey Dee and the Starlighters and the bright, bouncy music filled the room. Linda and Teddy resumed twisting their brains out.

Margaret Mary walked me over to the sofa. We sat down.

"We don't have to do this if you don't want to." She offered.

It wasn't that. I wanted to, sort of, but felt foolish, inhibited would have been the proper word, but I didn't want to disappoint Margaret Mary.

"No, I want to, I liked the slow ones, I just have to get used to the fast ones."

So we sat this one out as Joey Dee and the Starlighters knocked themselves out. When they finished Linda and Teddy came over and joined us on the sofa.

"You okay, you hurt yourself or something?" Teddy asked.

"No, I'm alright, just needed a break for a minute. You're doing real good Teddy, you too Linda."

"Teddy is a real good dancer," Linda replied, "its easy dancing with him." Teddy beamed. Linda smiled. Margaret Mary took my hand.

"David is getting better. He just hasn't found the fun yet."

And she was right, of course. Up till then fun for me was a line drive into the gap, or a jump shot that swished the basket, racing downhill on my bike, going from first to third on a liner into right field, snagging a pop up. Dancing was new, girls, at least dancing with girls, was new. I didn't know the rules, couldn't tell when I was doing well or messing up. Margaret Mary was right, I couldn't find the fun.

"You were doing good on the slow ones," Teddy offered, "and Maggie looked good on all of them."

Teddy had begun calling Margaret Mary "Maggie" a few weeks ago. After some initial resistance Margaret Mary had given in, realizing it was Teddy's way of expressing his friendship, but to me she would always, forever be Margaret Mary. And yes, she was a good dancer.

"Let's take a break for a minute. Does anyone want a Coke?" Margaret Mary offered. Does anyone ever not want a Coke? We moved into the kitchen and Margaret Mary brought four cold bottles to us at the kitchen table.

"Teddy, are you going to Lowell High this fall?" Linda asked.

Teddy was eighth grade like us, but not at the Immaculate. He was at the Moody School, an ancient, storied public school close to Shedd Park. The Moody had a ninth grade, unlike the Immaculate, which was the same as freshman year in high school. Students could choose whether to stay at the Moody or go to Lowell High. I hoped Teddy would be at Lowell High with me.

"Yeah, I'm going out for JV Baseball. Moody doesn't have a team."

Both Teddy and I were going to play in the Babe Ruth League for baseball this summer. Babe Ruth League is where you play after Little League. Big Diamond, big field, ages twelve through fifteen. We hadn't tried out yet, but both of us had done well in the Little League and I was sure we'd both make teams. Babe Ruth first, and after that maybe junior varsity at Lowell High.

"I can't wait to get to Lowell High," Linda added, "only thing wrong is Margaret Mary won't be there with us."

Not there with us? School without Margaret Mary? I had considered this, but not as a reality, until now. Margaret Mary was the reason I studied, why I wanted "A"'s like hers, instead of "B"s and "C"s like my buddies. She and I had done our homework together, studied for tests, gone to the library and eaten lunch together for three years. Won't be there with us?

Lowell had six parochial elementary schools like the Immaculate Conception where Margaret Mary and I had been in the same classrooms for three years. But Lowell had only two Catholic high schools, fed by the top students from the elementary schools. Each year, at the end of the eighth grade there was a city wide entrance exam, the results of which admitted the chosen few to Keith Academy for boys or Keith Hall for girls. Selection was considered a high honor in the city, the best and the brightest. For the rest there was Lowell High. Margaret Mary was a shoe-in for Keith Hall, she was the best and brightest and they would be lucky to have her.

"I'm not so sure I won't be at Lowell High this fall", Margaret Mary replied,

"I may not go to Keith Hall even if I do get in."

"Why on earth not?" Linda said, "That's where all the smart kids go."

"Yeah," Teddy added, "Dave's always telling me you're wicked smart."

 "I haven't made my mind up yet and my father says I can go wherever I want. I'm going to have to think about it a lot, but I really don't want to talk about it now. Let's finish our Cokes and dance some more, alright?"

And she shot me a look that meant we'd talk more about this later. Meanwhile it was back to the dance floor.

"Let's try a faster one," Linda said as she dropped "Please Mr. Postman" by The Marvellettes on the turntable. The music was bright and bouncy so I tried to be bright and bouncy. Once again I felt like an idiot.

"No, no, no," Margaret Mary said gently, "Not so fast, just listen to the music and do what I do."

So I watched and I listened, and I still felt like an idiot when I tried to bounce around. Mercifully, "Please Mister Postman" ended. Teddy and Linda were all smiles. Margaret Mary looked concerned.

"What do you want to hear next?" Linda asked while rummaging through our record pile.

"Let's do another fast one!" Teddy exclaimed with great enthusiasm.

"David," Margaret Mary asked, "What would you like to dance to?"

"I kind of like the Everly Brothers. Do we have anything by them?"

"Yes", Linda answered pulling a record from the pile. Then "Bye Bye Love" filled the room. Teddy and Linda were off and running. Margaret Mary waited patiently for me to start moving.

"Just relax, listen to the music and move along with it." She whispered as she started to dance. I began slowly, trying to do what she was doing, feeling only slightly less self-conscious because I liked the record so much. Then it happened, somehow I was moving with the music and I could see a smile on Margaret Mary's face as we danced along. In all too short a time the record ended.

"My turn," Teddy announced putting another record on the turntable. Dion DiMucci's "The Wanderer" strutted forth and once again I followed Margaret Mary's lead, feeling almost relaxed.

So our Saturday afternoon dance party went on. By the time three o'clock rolled around I was almost having fun. I had mastered, sort of, the slow ones. I knew I could count on ballads by Roy Orbison, Connie Francis, The Shirelles, Gene Pitney and The Drifters. I could get by, sort of, when Elvis started rockin', Duane Eddy started twangin', or Little Richard started wailing. I never got used to The Twist though, felt like an idiot, looked like an idiot.

Teddy on the other hand was an ace. He danced well, better than well, and both Linda and Margaret Mary took turns dancing all over the room with him. I was never going to be a good dancer, Teddy was always going to be an excellent one. As we walked home that afternoon I felt a sense of satisfaction, as well as relief, that it was over. I was glad I had Teddy with me for the experience and even with my awkwardness felt we had both had learned our lessons well.

"That Linda is kind of pretty, don't you think?" Teddy asked.

"Yeah, and you guys were really good dancers."

"You were doing good on the slow ones." Teddy replied.

"Yeah, but not so good on the fast ones."

"Or the almost fast ones." Teddy teased. "You kind of looked like you were on fire and trying to put yourself out."

"Did not!" And Teddy skipped away as I took a playful swing at him.

"I can't wait to do it again, like at a dance or something." Teddy said as we resumed our walk home.

And there it was, dances were now in the conversation. Record hops at the Commodore Ballroom or the Immaculate CYO Hall, Disc Jockey parties at the York Beach Casino, the Frolics at Salisbury Beach, and all places the big kids went were now on our platter. Teddy seemed a lot more at ease with the idea than I was.

"I think you gotta be in high school to go to dances." I offered.

"Yeah, but after this summer we will be in high school."

High school. Dances. Dances with girls. Dates. Another page was turning, another chapter beginning. Things were starting to get complicated. And scary. Then I had a thought.

"Hey Teddy", I said with just the right amount of self-satisfaction in my voice, "we know how to dance."

Teddy looked at me for a moment, than a big smile came across his face.

"Whadd'ya mean we?" Teddy replied as he danced home.

It's gotta be rock and roll music, if you wanna dance with me.

— *Chuck Berry* —

Chapter 10

THE GAME

As I stepped into the batter's box at O'Donnell Field I looked out over the infield. I could see Teddy hopping around off second base trying to annoy the pitcher as much as possible so I could get a good pitch. Teddy had doubled to lead off the bottom of the seventh inning in a six to six tie ballgame with the Cubs.

Peter Adams, our second baseman had struck out after Teddy reached base and Larry Wyman popped out to third just before me. So with two out and runner in scoring position it was up to me to get Teddy home. Babe Ruth ballgames were only seven innings and could end in a tie so this was our last chance, all or nothing. Cool.

Me and Teddy had both tried out for the Babe Ruth League earlier that summer and were thrilled to find we both made the same team, the best, the Red Sox, together. Now on a hot summer night in late June I was right where I wanted to be, doing exactly what I wanted to do. For me, on this summer night long ago, baseball was the best, the shiniest, the perfect place for me to be. How often does that happen?

Frankie Myers out in left field was playing way too shallow and if I got the right pitch I knew I could put one over his head and get Teddy home. Jack Lynch, playing third, was staying too close to the line in case Teddy broke for third base. The second baseman was cheating toward second base hoping to get Teddy picked off. This made a big hole on the right side of the infield. If I got an outside pitch I could punch a ground ball through that hole and also get Teddy home. Ball on the inside of the plate I drill over the left fielder's head, outside, I punch one into right field. Either way I was getting Teddy home. I stepped up to the plate took a practice swing and dug in.

All around me, off the field, things were changing, rapidly, almost daily. What used to be wasn't, things I had grown comfortable with, school, friends, family, all had become different, strange, more complicated. Baseball was the one constant, the same game, regular, dependable, safe. Fun.

Three short weeks ago the jolting changes descended. First was our well-choreographed and semi-solemn eight grade graduation ceremony. Caps, gowns, diplomas and lots of smiles and congratulations. And of course there was a card, lots of cards actually, they were nice. No more grade school now, high school, the big campus, beckoned in the fall. And then there was the dance, a record hop for us graduates.

I went with Margret Mary, naturally, but she made it very clear I could dance with whoever I wanted and that she would do the same. So when we got there Margaret Mary joined the girls on one side of the hall while I stood around with the guys on the other side. When the music started nothing much happened. None of the boys made any effort to cross the room and ask a girl to dance and I sure as heck wasn't going to be the first, or even the second for that matter. Eventually a few of the girls began dancing together on the fast records, among them Margaret Mary. I felt like I should get over there and ask her to dance and finally took a deep breath and started across the dance floor. When I got about two steps out the record started, Chubby Checker, Twisting Again, Like He Did Last Summer. I turned around and rejoined the herd of guys. Margaret Mary was twisting away with Linda Rogers and I could see the smile on her face when she saw me spin around and retreat. Not much got past Margaret Mary.

Eventually I did cross the floor. I danced with Margaret Mary and then Linda Rogers and even with Barbara Mitchell, the prettiest girl in our class. I even remembered to tell Margaret Mary how pretty she looked but didn't mention how jealous I felt when she danced with Paul Sanders from our class three times. Dances were complicated, girls were getting complicated, and school was going to an all new level, only baseball remained the same, safe at home.

Steve Roman, the Cubs pitcher, had this big, junky curveball he liked to throw because he thought it was cool. Trouble was he couldn't throw it hard enough to get it by anybody. The ball had a nice enough hook on it, but it hung like a balloon after it broke. If he dangled it over the plate I was going to hit it a mile. I watched Steve get set to pitch and at the last possible moment I asked for time and stepped out of the batter's box. I wanted Steve to pitch when I wanted him to, not when he wanted to.

As I backed off the plate I tugged at my shirt and waved the bat around a little I knew Steve was getting more and more annoyed out on the mound.

Good. Annoyed pitchers make mistakes. I hit mistakes.

As I stepped back into the batter's box I glanced over at my Mom and Dad who were on the sidelines along with my two brothers. Mom was talking to Frankie Myers' mother but my Dad gave me the swing level and hard sign and clapped his hands. There was lots of chatter on the field and our coach, Joe Skeehan, gave me the swing away sign.

My Babe Ruth games were family affairs, usually followed by ice cream at Nichols Dairy as we recapped the game. Teddy rode to the games with us and was usually part of the post-game activity unless Chris roared up on his motorcycle and swept a glowing Teddy up for a ride home. Hot summer nights, baseball in the park, homemade ice cream at a family dairy farm, swing away? You bet I would.

Steve Roman bounced the first pitch up to the plate. Ball one. He went into his windup again and I knew right away, here comes the curve ball, high arc, big twist of his wrist, another one into the dirt. Ball two. Hitters count, he better throw a strike here if he didn't want to walk me. Then the catcher called time and walked out to the mound for a conference. As the talk on the mound went on I stepped out again and looked over the field. Teddy had a huge grin on his face, he was having as much fun as I was.

A week after the graduation dance the second bombshell hit. To my utter dismay I passed the Keith Academy entrance exam. I was one of the chosen few, the elite, who would attend Lowell's finest, (and only) Catholic High school for boys. My parents and family were very proud of me, Margaret Mary was thrilled as well. Me, not so much. First of all I chafed against having a test decide where I was going to high school, or what I would become, or how I would get there. Even then, way back in my no longer in the eighth grade brain I disliked, intensely, elitism and Keith Academy had a considerable amount of snobbery attached. I wanted Lowell High, where my Dad and Mom had gone, with Teddy and my buddies, relaxed and casual, teenaged, not young adult. But I did not want to let my parents down, Margaret Mary thought it was a good idea, kind of, and I wanted to do the right thing. Keith Academy it was going to be, kind of.

"I'm not sure Keith Hall is where I want to go either," Margaret Mary said, "but I think we should try it for a year and see how it is. Remember, they're not trying us out, we're trying them out."

That made sense, kind of, and I had never gone wrong listening to Margaret Mary before so I agreed. Yet deep inside I had a feeling this was not going to go well, at least for me.

The conference on the mound broke up and the ballgame got back under way. Teddy bounced around some more, Steve went into his windup, and a huge meatball of a curve floated up to the plate.

I swung as hard as I could, felt the solid smack of the ball on the bat and knew I had hit it right on the screws. The ball rocketed into left field, high and mighty, over Frankie's head and soaring for the warning track. I watched the ball arc away for just a moment and then took off for first base. Teddy was off at the crack of the bat from second. He rounded third full speed before I got to first where I made a big turn and dug for second. Frankie Myers was back peddling madly as the ball hung up in the night summer air. I stopped at second as Teddy crossed the plate with the winning run. I watched Frankie turn and try to run under my fly ball, looking back over his shoulder in what I was sure was a futile effort to catch up. Teddy was standing at home plate clapping and my teammates had cleared the bench and were clapping and dancing about too. Then Frankie stretched out, dove and somehow, unbelievably, caught the ball. It was, by far, the greatest catch I had ever seen. I was dumbfounded, standing on second base with my mouth open. As my team mates grew silent, Frankie's went over the moon. They were all jumping around, pounding each other on the back, running out on the field to celebrate with Frankie.

Frankie had fallen over backwards after catching my ball and as he slowly got back on his feet he looked in his glove as if he too was surprised to find the ball in there. I walked off second base shaking my head as Frankie's teammates rushed past me. Teddy was still standing at home plate where his run didn't count. The game was over, tied at six. No winner today, and no loser either. I couldn't have hit the ball any harder. Frankie could not have made a better catch. That, for me, is the beauty of baseball, sometimes, some magical times, there are no winners or losers, just the players, playing.

When the crowd around Frankie broke up I walked over to the Cubs bench. His team mates parted as I got there and I held my hand out to Frankie.

I started to tell him what a great catch that was but I couldn't because we both started to laugh at the same time. All I could say was "Wow!" Frankie nodded his head and said "Wow!" too.

Just like when the Eskimos got into heaven.

Keith Academy, Lowell Massachusetts

Chapter 11

BOOLA-BOOLA

"Never mind why! You do not need to know why! You are here to learn how to determine the area of an equilateral triangle, not why!"

"Beaky" Bolton was fuming, again. He was my freshman year Geometry teacher at Keith Academy. He was also a bully, a weasel and a very poor teacher. We called him Beaky because he had a big nose and we didn't like him. He called us stupid because we didn't care much about parallelograms and he didn't like us. How does a guy like that get into teaching anyway?

I was six weeks into my freshman year at Keith Academy and things were going worse than my lowest expectations. Most of the teachers were Xaverian Brothers, kind of like guy nuns. A few of them were okay but for the most part they were more interested in what we could memorize and repeat back to them than what we were learning.

I could tell you without hesitation that The Battle of Hastings took place in 1066 without the slightest clue as to who fought there or why or even where Hastings was. I could conjugate verbs in Latin, name, with some hesitation the 12 Apostles, and figure the square root of 163. Never mind WHY.

Less than two months in and I already led my class in after school detention, sixteen and counting. Most of this punishment I brought upon myself as I discovered a new found resistance to authority which initially revealed itself when I decided I had little or no respect for Keith Academy's methods. Corporal punishment was the go to option for arresting the attention of restless, bored, overheated thirteen year olds in stuffy, antiquated classrooms. The place had more than enough smacking with rulers, pinching of ears and cracks to the head for disciplining students. Couple that with an ingrained sense of entitled snobbishness among the students and I was worse off than any fish out of water. I was in the wrong place at the wrong time with the wrong attitude. Correctly.

The trouble started during freshman orientation week when smug upper classman took it upon themselves to generally harass and bully us freshman. Meanwhile distant, dictatorial teachers laid down the law about what was expected of us as "Keith Academy Material". Initially my plan was to get in middle and shut up but my cover was blown, no kidding, when one of the Brothers Xaverian deciding he did not like the way I combed my hair. Yeah, my hair combing was not up to his, and apparently the school's standards. I was warned, in front of the whole class, then punished with after school detention, for unruly hair, then threatened with further sanctions. So I dug in.

I read the school rules, carefully, no mention or guidelines for hair combing, just arbitrary interpretation of a teacher's whims. Upper classman seemed to receive more leeway in this department but freshman, like myself, were fair game for a host of petty, capricious criticisms.

While I was being vilified for my hair other of my classmates were being singled out for the way they dressed, or spoke, or ate their lunches. I even saw one hapless freshman, Terry Nelson, brought to tears by a teacher who didn't approve of the way he walked! These harangues were not building character, they were destroying self-esteem. Yet worst of all, for me, was the enthusiastic endorsement of these unnecessary humiliations by the upper classman. Students against students. It was going to be a long year.

Incidentally, the student being berated by Beaky Bolton about equilateral triangles was my pal, Peter Rayburn from the Immaculate who had expanded his repertoire of confrontational inquiries to include Geometry and other school topics. "Why" was what Peter wanted to know most of all and I had increasingly come to admire his stance enough to sign on myself and become far less apt to accept as rote whatever our teachers were spouting. I saw a lot of Peter in Detention Hall.

"You wore the pheasant tie again, didn't you?" Margaret Mary asked, half accusing, half knowing.

"Yeah", I replied, more than a little self-satisfied.

"And you got detention for it, right?"

"Three detentions, they said one wasn't making the proper point with me anymore."

I should explain about the pheasant tie. Keith has this rule, students must wear a sport coat and tie to school every day. It's in the rule book, take it or leave it. One day I came to school wearing a string tie, like the cowboys wore, that my father had given me. I thought it was cool. Brother Patrician, Keith's headmaster, disagreed. He made me take it off and wear a paper tie in school that day. Sort of like a dunce cap only around your neck. The school rule book said you had to wear a tie, no mention of no string ties, so I wore one. That day and the next day. That got me another of many detentions. Also I was told if I wore it again I would be sent home for the day. They called my parents and that put an end to my string tie experience. Then I found the pheasant tie.

Hanging in my father's closet was a tie, unworn for decades, which had belonged to my grandfather. It was a bright turquoise blue, four inches wide in the middle with a hand painted, rhinestone flying pheasant taking to flight. The minute I saw it I couldn't wait to see what Brother Patrician thought of this one. The war of wills I couldn't possibly win was on.

The first day I wore it I was called to the front of the class and ridiculed by the teacher as my classmates laughed at me. I didn't care. Ridicule and the approval of my classmates mattered not a bit to me. I was sent to the Principal's office where I was threatened with the paper tie. I argued that the tie was a gift from my grandfather and I wore it in his memory. Surprisingly Brother Patrician bought this even though I had made the whole story up. I figured if they could tell stories about Jesus walking on water and raising the dead, not to mention the loaves and fish tale, I could assemble a whopper about my grandfather. It worked. I went back to class. No paper tie, but a lot of attention from each of my teachers for the rest of the day. It was strongly suggested by several of my teachers that I not wear the tie any more. Suggested, not ordered. I wore it the next day and the next and that started a lengthy string of detention hall visits.

"Are you trying to get yourself expelled?" Margaret Mary asked.

"I'm trying to get them to follow the rules they keep telling us we have to follow." I replied, only half sure I was telling the truth.

"Well they are not going to follow the rules, they are the rules. You are going to get yourself expelled." Margaret Mary said, with a hint of exasperation in her voice.

"Yeah, I sure hope so. I can't stand that place."

"Then you should leave on your terms, not theirs. If they kick you out, they win. If you don't want to go there ask your Mother and Father to let you transfer to Lowell High. Then you're leaving because you want to, not because they are making you. That's what I'm going to do."

"You're not going to stay at Keith Hall?"

"Everything you say about Keith Academy is true about Keith Hall, only worse. All the nuns seem to want us to become are good little housewives with three Catholic children and a clean house."

Margaret Mary was getting up a head of steam. "The only thing worse than the teachers is the other girls. All they are concerned about is whether they are going to wear lipstick on Saturday night and who is going to ask them to dance at the Commodore."

This was keep quiet time for me, Margaret Mary was not done yet. Like I said before, I was learning. "The worst part of all is that they don't seem to care if we learn anything or not. The teachers and the students. The teachers just want us to be good girls, the girls just want to be liked by the teachers and their boyfriends!"

Margaret Mary was starting to stomp around a little bit. I stayed quiet and paid attention.

"There's this girl there that I really like. Her name is Rose Nowack. She wants to be a doctor, like her father. The nuns told her being a doctor is for men, and what she should really do is become a nurse. I almost screamed!"

"You know how you're always telling me to calm down when I get too excited about something", I interrupted cautiously, very cautiously, and before I could continue Margaret Mary took a deep breath and did just that, calmly.

"I am going to finish freshman year there and then transfer to Lowell High in the fall. When I leave I am going to have the highest grades in my class and have the best record of all the freshman girls. And when they ask me why I am leaving I am going to tell them and they will have to listen."

This made sense. Margaret Mary usually made sense but this was not the way my school year was going to play out. I was going to continue to bait the tiger, Peter Rayburn was going to continue to ask why and Beaky Bolton was going to continue to cram confounding Geometry down our throats. Latin verbs were going to continue to be conjugated, Gospels, which were beginning to sound more like fairy tales every day, would continue to be studied and sanctified and I was going to go a little longer between haircuts.

I decided that if I couldn't beat the system at least I could make it sweat a little. And wear any kind of tie I wanted.

Chapter 12

NOT SKIING TRIP

When I found Margaret Mary in the cold night air she was crying her eyes out.

"Go away!" She sobbed while hiding her face in the shadows.

"No." I stood my ground, waiting.

"I mean it! Go away, I don't want you here right now."

"I don't care how mad you get at me, or how many times you tell me to go away, I'm staying right here because I want to help."

"You can't help! Just go away and leave me alone."

"No."

This whole scene was playing out on the second night of our CYO Ski Trip to Mount Snow, in Dover, Vermont in the frosty, snowy winter of 1962.

Once a year the Immaculate Conception Church would host a weekend ski trip for young parishioners. There were ski lodge dormitories for the girls and boys, lots of chaperones and watchdogs for the attendees and brilliant plans by those same attendees to circumvent all of the above.

The trip cost fifty dollars, a huge sum in those days, which I had obtained by making the trip part of my Christmas presents and through my ongoing career as a neighborhood snow shoveler with Teddy.

There were forty of us kids on the trip, about even girls and boys, along with the adult supervision and spiritual overseers. We left by chartered bus from the school yard at four o'clock on Friday afternoon and would return Sunday evening after six. In between there would be lots of shenanigans, horseplay, drama and even a little skiing on the outing. I had never been on skis in my life, really didn't plan to either, but I really wanted to go on the trip. Margaret Mary was going, and Peter Rayburn, and a whole bunch of my other friends. To me this was an adventure, the first time I would be away from home without my family. This wasn't about skiing, it was about getting out there, into the world on my own. Sort of.

Margaret Mary stopped crying and turned to face me. Even in the shadows I could see that her eyes were red and puffy from her tears and that her nose was all red, and running.

"Here's a hanky, it's clean."

I passed her my handkerchief and took a step back so she could come out of the shadows. Margaret Mary blew her nose and folded the handkerchief carefully before handing it back to me.

"Thank you", she whispered and then looked me in the eye.

"I feel like such a fool."

"How come?" I asked, stepping closer and trying to take her hand.

Just then a group of kids came pouring out of the lodge to have a snowball fight in the courtyard. Margaret Mary ducked back into the darkness until the group passed us by.

"Walk with me a little bit please." She asked and we headed for a snow covered bench at the far end of the courtyard away from the snowballers. Then she slipped her hand into mine as we sat down.

"I am acting like such a fool." She began.

"You already said that", I offered, hoping to lighten the mood. Instead I got a cross look from Margaret Mary.

"Last night I let Paul Sanders kiss me." She said, I reeled, she continued. "Today I saw him holding hands with Nancy Hackett."

Although I wasn't quite done reeling yet I knew this was the time for some sort of positive comment on my part. I had none.

"I hate it that I'm acting just like all those other silly girls from school."

"Maybe," I knew I might be stepping of a ledge here, but I had to say something, Margaret Mary really seemed upset, "Maybe it's not silly, maybe you just got your feelings hurt." Like mine were, now.

"I know, but I still feel like a fool."

"Because you let him kiss you?"

"No, because I thought it meant something when he did."

Well I was really out of my league now. You see up to this point I had never really kissed a girl. I knew that I was going to get around to it, and I wanted to, but so far I hadn't. Silence reigned on our snowy park bench as across the courtyard a lively snow ball fight was in full session. "Well I don't think you're a fool," I finally offered, "you are the least like a fool person I know."

Margaret Mary squeezed my hand and then moved closer to me and put her head on my shoulder. "I don't think I'll ever let anybody kiss me ever again." She sighed.

"Now you do sound like a fool." And I tossed some of the light, newly fallen snow into her face. Margaret Mary sprang up off the bench and chased me as I took off running.

When she caught me, as she had long before this chase had ever begun, we laughed and hugged and a few minutes later we joined the group in the snowball fight.

"The first time you fall in love, it changes you forever, and no matter how hard you try, that feeling just never goes away."

Nicholas Sparks

Jacqueline Kennedy White House, Feb. 14, 1962

Chapter 13

HEARTS & FLOWERS & WALLPAPER

It was Valentine's Day night, one month after my ski trip adventure and once again there is a gathering in our living room for yet another first of its kind television special.

As in many thousands of other American homes, TV watching had become a glowing, mesmerizing nightly ritual for my family. Cops and robbers, cowboys and Indians, Red Skelton, Jack Benny and Jackie Gleason were now regularly scheduled performers in our home. Slowly, surely, inevitably, TV was becoming what we did instead of reading, playing card or board games or even talking to one another about the events of the day or the cares and concerns of our lives.

There were guidelines of course, at least in my home. Homework had to be done and checked over by my Dad before the TV was turned on. Nine o'clock was school night bedtime, ten, sometimes even eleven on weekends. Saturday morning cartoons were to be played on low volume and were limited to two hours, usually eight till ten, before my brothers and I were relegated to the backyard or the playground or anywhere outside where we would not be in the house, making a mess.

Each of us had our favorites, Matt Dillon, Walt Disney, Lassie and Ralph Kramden were must see guests, along with The Rifleman, Ed Sullivan and Dobie Gillis. On Friday nights we were allowed to stay up later, which allowed us to watch 77 Sunset Strip or the Bell Telephone Hour until Rod Serling arrived, cigarette in hand, to guide us into The Twilight Zone.

TV had become, above all else, diverting, entertaining, distracting and even occasionally an educational part of our family interaction. As was the case tonight when Jacqueline Kennedy would take America on a guided tour of the White House on which she had recently overseen a two million dollar restoration. President Kennedy would remain tactfully off stage as this spotlight was for the reigning Queen of Camelot, our First Lady, and, at least in our neck of the woods, the most admired woman in America.

Only 31 years old when she entered the White House, Jaqueline Bouvier Kennedy had entranced the nation with her soft spoken elegance, poise and beauty. As photogenic as her movie star Presidential husband, her hairstyle, wardrobe and manners had become the touchstone for a whole generation of women and young ladies striving to carve a more definitive place for themselves in the period's largely male dominated society. No finer authority than Margaret Mary herself had assured me that Jackie Kennedy represented all that a modern woman should be and was herself the woman she hoped she would become.

Jack Kennedy often noted that when making a public appearance with his wife there were many more people interested in her wardrobe than what he had to say. And together they made a glowing, graceful pair of role models for our country and the world.

So on this night in our living room Margaret Mary was there, of course, though Sean was absent, regretfully attending a faculty meeting at the college. Both she and my Mom were seated front row center as this was primarily a ladies night event and though my Dad and I were wondering if Cheyenne Bodie was shooting anyone interesting in the Old West, we too were anxious to witness the unveiling of the new White House and learn a bit more about our President's wife. My two brothers were in the bedroom pouting because they couldn't watch Zorro.

The program was being run on two of the three major networks simultaneously and rerun by the third the following night. It would attract an audience of over 56 million viewers, a huge showing for the time. The program, broadcast in black and white and co-hosted by ABC news personality Charles Colingwood, was a dazzling success, showcasing the elegant and refined First Lady as well as the regal refurbishment of the White House building and grounds.

"Doesn't she look wonderful?" Margaret Mary commented while riveted to the TV screen.

"Very nice, and those rooms! She did such a marvelous job of decorating." My Mother added.

"Must have cost a fortune." My Dad added.

Although I was still wondering how Cheyenne Bodie was doing I too couldn't help being impressed, no charmed, by the evenings telecast. As our First Lady glided from room to room offering insights and background to the portraits, furnishings and historical significance of her surroundings her sense of grace and dignity shone from the screen into our fully appreciative living room.

Ever since his inauguration President Kennedy and his family had risen to become American Royalty, instilling a renewed sense of pride and purpose, hope and confidence in the leadership of the nation. Like rock and roll, President and Mrs. Kennedy represented youth rising, a glittering future ahead, commitment to lofty ideals and social progress, all things possible and wrapped up in the style and grace Jacqueline Kennedy was showing us this evening.

"This summer Sean and I are going to go to Washington and see the White House and visit the museums." Margaret Mary announced as a commercial break in the program began.

An instant pang of envy raced through me at the thought. Visit Washington? Really? The idea seemed as far-fetched to me as a trip to the moon. My world at this point stretched as far north as York Beach, Maine and as far south as Boston, thirty miles away. Any further than that was beyond my reasoning, something other people did perhaps, but not yet part of my allowable expectations.

'How are you going to get there? Are you gonna take a plane?" Another of my unimaginable yearnings.

"By bus, Sean said we can get there by Greyhound Bus right from down city."

"Next to Kresge's, the bus depot." My Dad added helpfully

"That should be quite and adventure," My Mom said wistfully.

"Does anybody want anything from the kitchen?"

Dad and I said no but Margaret Mary followed my mother into the kitchen.

"Where is the furthest away from home you've ever been Jackie?" Mom had insisted Margaret Mary call her by her first name. They were friends.

"I have relatives in Canada, Quebec City. I used to go and visit them when I was a little girl."

"But you don't go anymore?"

"Being married and having three kids makes traveling much more difficult."

Margaret Mary pondered that thought as my Mother poured steaming water into a teapot. Then she asked, "Is being married a good thing?"

My Mom stopped pouring and considered her answer carefully. "Of course it is, in many ways. Dave is a wonderful husband and provider, I love the boys, but," And then she looked to the living room door and lowered her voice, "You give up a lot of yourself once you start a family."

"Do you miss being not married?" Margaret Mary asked.

"Sometimes, not often. When I'm very tired and there is still lots to do around the house I wish I could just sit and read a book, or go to a movie by myself, take a walk, things like that."

"But most of the time you like it?" Margaret Mary asked, sounding like she was trying to sell herself something.

"Most of the time yes, I do. But I often miss those 'some of the times'." My Mom placed the teapot and cups on a tray and headed back to the living room, Margaret Mary following.

On the TV Jackie Kennedy had taken the program outside the White House to the newly replanted Rose Garden. As she and Mr. Collingwood walked the grounds Mom served tea.

"Do you think maybe someday we could go there Dad?" I asked, Margaret Mary's announced trip still ringing in my ears.

"We'll see", my Dad replied accepting a cup of tea from my Mom.

'We'll see', was a go to answer for a lot of my requests, not exactly a no, but certainly not a yes and far more polite than forget about it, which is what 'We'll see' usually implied.

"It would be nice to take the kids to see the White House." My Mother offered.

"It would be nice to be able to afford to take the kids to see the White House." My Dad responded. Touche'.

Money, or the lack thereof, was neither a frequent nor public issue in our home. Perhaps it was a sensitive behind closed doors topic for my parents, something was. But the matter seldom came up and when it did it had little effect on me or my brothers. I certainly never felt deprived, though the commercial world displayed an endless array of newer, shinier, trendier products guaranteed to make our lives happier. Like coonskin caps and Radiant Cooked Hot dogs.

Jackie Kennedy concluded the program by thanking viewers for watching and reminding us that the treasures of the White House belonged to us, the American people to take pride in and appreciate. As she spoke our living room chatter died down as we turned our full attention to her. And that is where the Magic lay.

President and Mrs. Kennedy had instilled in the American public a tremendous sense of national pride, of belonging, and a will to change things for the better as the future raced toward us. Six days after this broadcast we put our third man into space, Gus Grissom, Apollo Astronaut and National Hero. Such was the sense of the times, National Pride and National Heroes, with much more of both promised.

Through the magical window of television and the mesmerizing charisma of our President and First Lady all good things seemed possible, all challenges could be met, all obstacles overcome. And maybe, just maybe, we would take that trip to Washington, D.C. to see it all first hand. We'll see.

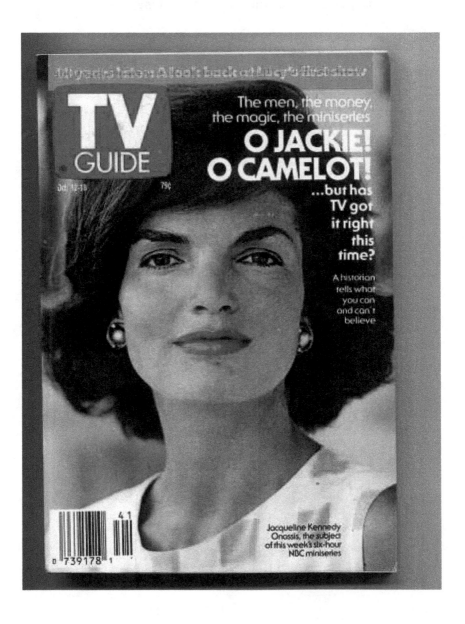

"Suddenly everything that had been a liability before, your hair, that you spoke French, you didn't just adore the campaign, everyone thought I was a snob and hated politics... And when we got in the White House all the things that I had always done suddenly became wonderful."

Jacqueline Kennedy

Chapter 14

NOT BOOLA-BOOLA

"They're kicking us out."

Peter Rayburn stammered as he left Brother Patrician's office. He passed me on the stairs without saying another word. It was the last day of the school year, June, 1962. I had finished my freshman year at Keith Academy in subdued fashion, giving up in fitting in, or being accepted, but determined to fly under the radar long enough to walk away from this school on my own terms over the summer. I was waiting for the last day of school bell to ring when I was called, once again, to the Principal's Office.

This was not an unusual occurrence for me, more like one more gathering of the Usual Suspects regarding some unresolved infraction of the myriad school rules. I wasn't particularly worried as I climbed the stairs to the principal's office until I saw the look on Peter Rayburn's face as he came out. Peter's words hit me like a hammer. I hadn't expected this. After a stormy start I had, somewhat reluctantly, cleaned up my act following my talk with Margaret Mary back during my pheasant tie period.

Heeding her advice I retired the magnificent rag and resorted to a non-descript rayon, clip on number I would normally have been totally ashamed of. I had even taken to applying a dab of Brylcreem to my hair, bringing me within the unspoken parameters of Keith Academy grooming standards. I did these things not by way of seeking forgiveness but for paving the way for my own exit strategy. I wanted out but I wanted out on my terms, not theirs.

Unsure of what to do next I waited in the hallway outside Brother Patrician's office. I was no stranger to the hallway or to the headmaster's office but this time was different, endgame. My feelings raced from fear to embarrassment to anger and back again uncertain as I was of the outcome of this confrontation. Then Mrs. Hodges, the school secretary, beckoned me into the office. She never looked at me as I walked past her desk.

"Master Ferrier, I have called you here this morning to inform you that you will not be allowed to re-enroll in this school in the fall."

Brother Patrician handed me a letter which I was pretty sure said what he had just said, only formally, to my parents. I took the letter and said, "I passed all my courses."

"Yes, you did. However your academic rating reflects that you are not achieving grades commensurate with your testing levels and further more you have had several disciplinary problems throughout this year."

My studies had never been a problem, I comprehended and grasped what I felt was relevant and buckled under to the rest. The notion of leaving this school on my terms was my plan and I applied myself to that goal. In vain.

"Maybe I'm not achieving grades commensurate with my testing levels because some of my teachers aren't doing a very good job of teaching." I might be going but I was not going quietly.

"I have a great deal of confidence in my faculty Master Ferrier. Suffice it to say that we have determined that you are simply not Keith Academy material."

As those words burned themselves into my forever brain I struggled to hold my temper and my tongue. One thing I had learned very well at Keith Academy was that it took a lot of planning and patience to fight the system and getting into a yelling contest with this guy was not going to work in my favor.

"I passed all my courses." I repeated stubbornly.

"That is true," Brother Patrician repeated in his most condescending voice, "Academics are not the reason you are being dismissed."

"Then it's not me who failed," I replied, "It's you." And I turned and walked out of the office. Mrs. Hodges didn't look at me when I left.

As I emptied my school locker I noticed that Peter Rayburn's locker was already empty. Usually we walked home from school together but I didn't see him anywhere. I felt really bad for Peter. Despite his uninterrupted string of demands to know why, Peter was an excellent student, near the head of our class in Math and Science. His conflicts with authority were less subversive than genuine attempts to round out his understanding. Peter asked why so that he would comprehend more completely and accept more easily the concepts placed before us. Peter was not a rebel against the system, he was a rebel within it and had they recognized this both he, and the school, would have been better off.

But they were kicking us out, along with Billy Barone, a smart, happy, funny kid who was constantly being berated because he was overweight, Arthur Sarmento, whose days were numbered because he regularly got caught smoking in the schoolyard, and Jimmy Laurent, a star player who quit the freshman football team after a disagreement with the coach. There were several other familiar faces from my frequent Detention Hall visits who were also on the way out. All together seven of us were being expelled that morning and being sent home early on this last day of the school year. I wasn't looking forward to breaking this news to my parents. It was going to be a long weekend.

"No kiddin', they kicked you out?" Teddy asked. We had met up at Shedd Park. I hadn't gone home yet.

"Yeah, and tonight I have to tell my Mom and Dad." This I was not looking forward to.

"Well, you hated that place and now you don't have to go there anymore. You comin' to Lowell High this fall?"

"Yeah," I replied, the first bright thought of the day.

"Then we can go out for baseball together! That'll be great!" Teddy said with a big smile.

I hoped I could think of something else great to tell my parents about this. We had discussed my unhappiness with Keith Academy several times during the school year but these discussions usually ended with the school being right and me needing to amend my attitude.

"Do you think your Mom and Dad are going to be mad?" Teddy asked.

"Worse than that," I answered, "They're going to be disappointed."

My attendance at Keith Academy was a source of great pride for my parents. I was the first, and probably the only, member of my family who would ever have the chance to go there and admittance meant status, acknowledgment that I was one of the chosen few. My getting kicked out of Keith was letting them down, something I tried very hard not to do.

"Lowell High's not so bad," Teddy offered, "for a school."

In fact both my mother and father had graduated from Lowell High. My Dad had played football there and still had his red letter sweater tucked away in a cedar chest. My Mom sometimes spoke of going to school dances and her friends and her prom where she must have been the prettiest girl there. Most of my gang from Shedd Park was going there. Me and Peter Rayburn were the only two who ended up at Keith. Not any more.

"Anyway, I hope you don't get yelled at too bad by your Mom and Dad for getting kicked out. I'm glad you're going to be at Lowell High next year."

"Me too," I said, knowing their silence was going to be worse that any yelling.

"Hey, I gotta go help my Dad down at the garage. Teddy said, "Don't forget we got practice tomorrow over at O'Donnel field."

I waved to Teddy as he took off glad to be reminded that life was going to go on, and that there was always baseball to round out the rough spots. But I still had to break the news to my parents, after dinner tonight, and after I had talked this over with Margaret Mary.

When I got to her house Margaret Mary was waiting for me at the top of her porch stairs.

"I heard what happened." She announced, that hint of sadness once again in her voice. "Was it awful?"

"How did you find out?" I was genuinely puzzled.

"Billy Barone's sister goes to school with me. Is it true they expelled Peter too?"

"Yeah, he looked really surprised. I don't think he did anything that wrong either. I didn't see him after school. I hope he's alright."

"We should go over to his house later and make sure." Margaret Mary suggested. Margaret Mary always knew the right thing to suggest. "And how about you?" she added, "How do you feel?"

By now we were seated on her front porch as I struggled to put my feelings into words. "I really wanted to leave the way you said instead of being kicked out." was all I could express right then as a massive lump formed in my throat, and my eyes, without permission, began to fill with tears.

Margaret Mary moved closer to me on the porch swing and took my hand in hers. "Well you tried, I know you did and you know you did. Everything you didn't like about that place is still true and now you don't have to be there anymore."

I started to reply and choked on the lump in my throat. Margaret Mary squeezed my hand.

"I was even in their stupid Minstrel Show!" was all I could choke out. Margaret Mary laughed her wonderful laugh at that and in a moment I was laughing too, sort of. I've got to tell you about the Minstrel Show.

The Keith Academy Minstrel Show was an evening of vaudevillian entertainment performed by the student body and hosted, I swear to God, by six Senior Classmen in black-face who cavorted about the stage performing every Step N'Fetchit, Amos and Andy, Mammy routine they could muster. Incredible as this may seem this embarrassingly racist nonsense was what the Keith Academy Hierarchy felt was part of a smashing night's entertainment. Keith Academy Material indeed.

Remember this is 1962. A young black minister named Martin Luther King is garnering headlines all across the country as he championed the movement for Civil Rights and Equal Opportunity for black Americans. Freedom Riders are crisscrossing the rural South in attempts to ease segregation practices and register black voters, the United States Supreme Court had declared segregation on public transportation unconstitutional and the Department of Defense had recently ordered the complete desegregation of the Armed Forces. And Keith Academy still had its annual Minstrel Show.

The entire student body was required to perform. The freshman class, me among them, made up the backing chorus for the night's hijinks. When the senior, black-faced, "Endmen" were not cavorting about in shameful parody of black, white or anybody's culture, various members of the student body performed skits, sang songs, hummed, strummed and danced about the stage. I hated every mandatory minute of it. Peter Rayburn, demanding to know why we were required to do this nonsense, did too. We both buckled under, sang the songs and sacrificed a little more of our developing self-respect. The laughter on Margaret Mary's front porch faded and anger replaced angst as I recalled the events of the day.

At precisely this moment Sean arrived home and could sense something was amiss. Placing his leather book bag on the floor he took a seat across from us and asked, "Has tragedy befallen? Tell me what is wrong and how I can help." Sean always knew how to ask, and often, how to help.

"David has been expelled from Keith Academy," Margaret Mary began, "and tonight he has to tell his parents."

"And for what infraction have you been dismissed?" Sean asked.

I struggled to get my answer into words. It took several deep breaths and a hard swallow or two before I could answer, "I passed all my subjects."

"Surely that is not the reason they have acted so." Sean replied. I could feel Margaret Mary's eyes on me. I felt the gentle pressure of her hand in mine.

"They said I was not Keith Academy material." The words burned, then as much as they do today.

"And what, exactly, is this material you have been accused of not having?" Sean asked gently.

I didn't know then, as now, and the question remains unanswered. Keith Academy material could only be defined by the lack, my lack, according to them. I was sure it had something to do with conformity, acquiescence, obedience, but I was never then, and am not now, sure of to what. There was that often spoken, general air of "better than" that permeated the school, pompous entitlement among the students, but to what I was never sure they felt they were entitled to, or better than.

"I don't know", was all I could mutter miserably in response to Sean's question. But not knowing was the reason I came to Margaret Mary's house in the first place.

"Well, there was the tie," Margaret Mary offered.

"Would that be the magnificent flying bird cravat my daughter described to me in days past?" Sean asked with a smile. I could only nod my head in answer.

"Now ask yourself," Sean continued," why do you think you wore this ornament that started so much trouble?"

I started and stopped, trying to get my thoughts into words as Sean and Margaret Mary waited patiently. Finally I admitted, "I didn't like that they could make any rules they wanted and then not do what the rules said." This was as close as I could come to explaining where my futile war with Keith Academy had begun. But Sean knew more,

"But why the tie of many colors? Why that tie?"

"Because I," then my mind went blank, frustration raged as I couldn't explain why I did what I did.

"Because you wanted to obey your way?" Margaret Mary suggested.

"I didn't like them telling me what to do all the time."

"Perhaps being Keith Academy Material has something to do with not minding being told what to do all the time." Sean suggested.

"And maybe the material they are looking for is not what is best for you." Margaret Mary added.

"I passed all my subjects." Somehow it felt important that I remind everyone of that.

"This is not a matter of how smart you are David," Sean began,

"It is a matter of who you are." Margaret Mary squeezed my hand, "who I was" felt better than I had all day.

"I am going to tell you a story," Sean said," It is a story I have not shared even with my daughter herself up to now. But I think perhaps this would be a good time for her, and you, to hear it. First however I believe I will fortify myself with a pint of ale and perhaps a bottle of excellent cream soda for the two of you."

Once we were properly beveraged and resettled on the porch Sean began, "Many years ago when I was about the age you two are now I felt I had a calling to the priesthood." Sean sipped, Margaret Mary leaned forward and I was glad we were talking about something else besides me.

"When I had finished my middle school, this was back in Ireland by the by, I took myself to a seminary, Saint Patrick's College it was, in a village named Maynooth, near Dublin. My parents were very proud of me for doing so, for in my family one either became a priest or a scoundrel, not unlike my father, and having a son who was a priest would lay less heavily on their minds."

"You were going to be a priest?" Margaret Mary asked in wonder.

"So I believed at the time," Sean said, "but this was not destined to come to pass. I had no tie with a pheasant to show them," Sean continued with a smile, "but in short order I found I did not have enough of the gift of faith to persevere."

"You didn't get along with the other priests?" I asked.

"Nor they with me alas. Not only did we think differently, we believed differently, a distinction that mattered more as time went on."

"Did they kick you out?" I almost hoped as Margaret Mary kicked me in the shin.

"No", Sean laughed, "Though my departure was a fairly mutual decision. You see the good fathers wanted me to stay, wanted me to finish my studies and take the Holy Orders, but I could not. Much of what they taught and believed was beautiful and right for the way I wanted to live my life in this world, but on other matters we were worlds apart."

"Like what?" Margaret Mary asked urgently.

Sean took a deep draught of his ale before continuing. Our cream sodas sat untouched on the end table, and that hardly ever happens.

"Celibacy of the priesthood was one matter," Sean began, "but larger still was the unyielding and uncompromising belief that Catholicism was the only true religion and that all other beliefs were false or misguided."

"Like the Eskimos," I suggested to Margaret Mary.

"Also they taught that Keats was a wastrel, Joyce no better and Michael Collins a criminal."

I wasn't sure who Michael Collins was or what a wastrel was, but I did know that you didn't mess with Keats or Joyce with Sean.

"So you quit going there?" Margaret Mary asked.

"Resigned, much to the sorrow of my family, yet I had no other choice you see, who they wanted me to be I could never be, nor was I willing to pretend to be."

"Was everybody mad at you for quitting?" I asked.

"Some were, others were disappointed, some, including my Mother, understood."

"But not you father?" Margaret Mary asked.

"My father was a man of action, of strong words with the temper of the bloody Irish about him. No, he did not understand." Sean finished his ale and yearned for another.

"So what did you do?" Margaret Mary inquired.

"I came to America," Sean continued, "to Chicago where I entered Loyola University as a sophomore and met your mother as Divine Providence's proof I had done the right thing."

"Have you ever wished you hadn't quit and become a priest?" I asked.

"Never once," Sean responded, "And every time I look at that child of my heart sitting next to you I know the reason why. Now don't either of you move while I refresh my drink for I am going to tell you why I have shared this story with you when I come back."

Margaret Mary and I sat spellbound still ignoring our cream soda until Sean returned holding a fresh bottle of ale. "Now the reason I have told you this tale," Sean began, "is that you are both coming to an age where you must consider who it is you want to be instead of who other people, including myself, want you to be. This is very difficult, but I know both of you can do this. David, I know and you must certainly realize that Keith Academy Material is neither who you are nor who you want to be."

To this I nodded, once again feeling better than I had all day.

"Unfortunately the decision to leave all that behind was made for you and I know this hurts." Sean sipped his ale, I swallowed, hard. "However the outcome is the same, you are now free to be whomever it is you want to be and I know you will make that decision wisely."

Sean considered Margaret Mary who was uncharacteristically silent. "And you my darling daughter, I know you find yourself at a similar crossroads. I just want you to know that whatever your decision and whenever you make it, I shall respect and support your choice."

Now it was Margaret Mary's turn to swallow hard. "I know you will," she replied and fell silent once again. So in the fading afternoon sunlight Sean finished his ale, we our cream sodas and after this I made my way home.

Later that evening I broke the news to my Mother and Father and handed them the dreaded letter. I saw the look of disappointment cross my Father's face and sensed my Mother's unhappiness as well but these things passed quickly as I told them my side of the story and related what I had learned that afternoon on Margaret Mary's front porch.

Life did go on, Margaret Mary and I did go over to Peter Rayburn's house to see if he was okay, and he was, sort of. The next day I was at O'Donnel field taking grounders at third base and deciding deep inside, who I wanted to be.

Nubble Light, York Beach, Maine

Chapter 15

THE YORKS

York Beach, Maine lies sixty miles north of Lowell on the southernmost tip of Maine, just over the border from Portsmouth, New Hampshire and across the Piscataqua River. York Beach is part of a coastal community delightfully called "The Yorks", consisting of York Village, York Harbor, and York Beach. Each of "The Yorks" has a distinct, beguiling character, colonial hamlet, rustic harbor, family resort. I have spent many of the most enjoyable times of my life in The Yorks, mostly York Beach, and this is where I retreated in this summer of 1962, in the weeks after I got kicked out of Keith Academy.

News travels fast in a small town like Lowell, bad news even faster. So when me and Peter and Billy Barone and all the rest, were dismissed by the Xaverian brethren, the whole city, or what seemed like the whole city, knew about it by the end of the day. We were marked, each of us, not exactly as outcasts, but questionable. We must have done something to deserve this reprimand; authority still wore the mantle of infallibility in those times.

York Beach is, for me a haven, a sanctuary, a place where I could get away from and forget, for a short while, my hometown troubles and barely a teenager blues. It has a rhythm, pace and ambience all its own, summertime casual and seaside serene. I couldn't wait to get there.

 Every Friday evening during the summer months my Dad would roll into our driveway from his work around 6PM and the countdown would begin. We, being my brothers and I, along with an invited friend each, would be dutifully standing by on the front porch as my Dad arrived. We would be loaded down with our bed pillows, extra blankets, towels, change of clothing, sweater or jacket, and any beach gear which had survived the previous weekend. My Mom would be assembling groceries in the kitchen, big boxes of breakfast cereal, a couple gallons of milk, sandwich meat, usually bologna or pimento

loaf, loaves of wonderful Wonder bread, eggs and soup, Campbell's
Chicken Noodle and Tomato being family favorites.

Within five minutes my Dad would have gone into the house, changed
clothes, used the bathroom and reemerged, carrying grocery bags to
the car. We, the kids, would have already stuffed our belongings into
the back of the station wagon and climbed aboard. Ten minutes flat
and we were on the road to The Yorks, a ninety minute journey that
included a ten cent toll booth, an enormous, slowly cranking
drawbridge, and stops at several family run roadside produce stands
offering Maine grown blueberries, sweet sugar corn and ruby red
beefsteak tomatoes.

For the first few weeks after the Keith thing I felt like I was carrying a
great weight around. Anger and resentment served to smother my
deeper feelings of shame and humiliation. I tended to mope a bit,
alternately feeling sorry for myself or plotting fantastic schemes of
getting even with the Keith Academy hierarchy. Margaret Mary
usually talked me down out of that tree, suggesting that feeling bad
was natural, but feeling bitter was beneath me. I wasn't so sure about
that. I secretly began to savor the taste of bitter.

I had really been thrown for a loop with the Keith thing. It was not
only my first taste of rejection, it was my first realization of the power
the system had to impact my life. My friends and family had
remained by my side but everyone else seemed to have taken a step
back. I was "the guy who got kicked out of Keith" and a shadow had
fallen over me. Except in The Yorks. Here I could still be me before
the fall, nobody here knew or cared about what happened in Lowell,
we were at the beach, doing beach things, taking a time out.
So for this weekend trip I invited no friend to come along to The
Yorks. Teddy was going to work for his Dad at the garage, Margaret
Mary wanted to stay with Sean and I needed some time to myself
along the magical coast of Maine. When we left Lowell that Friday
evening we were one short of a full load, my brothers each had a
buddy with them. I needed some time alone in the Yorks.

My family had a small camping trailer parked permanently at Camp
Eaton, a beachside community in York Beach which has been in
operation since 1923. Three generations of the Wagner family have

hosted around two hundred campers every summer over Camp Eaton's thirty seven acres. It is a family destination, usually rented for the entire season by loyal patrons who became summer friends but winter strangers in the traditional rhythm of New England life.

The trailers at Camp Eaton, parked side by side, row on row, offered camaraderie by mere proximity. Young and old alike, exuberant or in repose, gathered here for the same reason, respite from the city, whatever 'other place' they came from, whatever other life they left behind. Summer days and summer nights, one weekend at a time, tendered solace and friendship, and they delivered.

Camp Eaton is right on Route 1A, the shoreline highway that parallels the rugged Maine coastline and the magnificent southern limit of Long Sands Beach. It was a place of campfire evenings, board games, cribbage and one pot family dinners blessed with an occasional boiled lobster, lots of steamed clams and chowder. Aside from the shellfish there were steaming pots of boiled sugar corn, fresh off the farm, 60 cents a dozen on the side of the road, along with Essem hot dogs in toasted buns. The blueberries we bought or gathered were as big as your thumb, popping open in thick pancakes and fluffy oven muffins. Tomatoes sprinkled with sea salt stuffed our cold cut sandwiches at meals further seasoned with laughter, happiness and contentment.

York's main beach, Long Sands, stretched alongside Route 1A for a little over a mile. Rock strewn along the edges, the two hundred yard tidal fall left flat, glistening sands all the way to the water's edge at lowest tide. The tide pools among the rocks collected tiny crabs, periwinkles, and sometimes starfish for our weekend treasure hunts. The entire panorama is overseen by beautiful Nubble Light, also known as Cape Neddick Light though I never knew anyone who called it that. "The Nubble" has been in operation since 1879, its winking red lantern was visible across the silvery night sea from our trailer, ever shining through the starry nights, its white tower soothing our sight through the golden summer days.

When we arrived at Camp Eaton on Friday evening we would unload the car as rapidly as we filled it, and then, we, the kids, would rush off to find our York Beach friends as my Mom assembled a Friday night dinner for us all. Later, after dinner had been gobbled and Saturday adventures planned, around a front yard campfire we would toast marshmallows, light sparklers and listen to stories from our Camp Eaton next trailer neighbor, Eldridge Porter.

Mr. Porter was a retired fireman from Worcester, Massachusetts. His wife, Emma, had died several years before and he now spent the entire summer in his compact trailer parked right next to ours. He would usually be sitting in a cane chair on his plank porch in the sunset hours as we arrived. "Hello to the Ferrier clan!" He would proclaim as we rolled in. Then, as we scurried about our arrival tasks he would rise and build a campfire, ready to be ignited when the night stars arrived.

Mr. Porter loved books as much as anyone I had ever known, and while he was familiar with my Mr. Twain, and Margaret Mary's poets and poetesses, he was more a man of Zane Grey and Edgar Rice Burroughs, Mickey Spillane and Isaac Asimov. His trailer was stuffed full of magical paperback adventures, available, with some mild censoring, to me whenever I wanted. Enticing, colorful soft covers depicted lurid gun molls, gun totin' cowpokes and far away planets.

Whenever he finished one of these books he would recite, with much enthusiasm, the whole story, punctuated with grunts and groans, gunshots and gasps for us around the campfire. Often my brothers and the others would go off to sleep or to catch fireflies during a story but I always stayed, spellbound, to the very end. Under those York Beach stars and around those campground campfires I was introduced to Sherlock Holmes, John Carter of Mars, Matt Helm and Wyatt Earp among a host of others. In his deep, lumbering tone he would recite…

In the shadows of the forest that flanks the crimson plain…by the side of the Lost Sea of Korus,…in the Valley Dor, beneath the hurtling moons of Mars speeding their meteoric way close above the bosom of the dying planet I crept stealthily along the trail of a shadowy form that hugged the darker places with a persistency that proclaimed the sinister nature of its errand.[5]

---

[5] Warrior of Mars, Edgar Rice Burroughs.

And I would be transported to the Red Planet, Barsoom, alongside John Carter as he "crept stealthily along the trail of a shadowy form".

Another time we would be transported to a dusty cowpoke bar room as in...*Tobacco smoke hung thick in a haze near the low ceiling of the Topanga Saloon...*[6]

And I would be in the smoky saloon, there among the cowboys, playing poker, I feel the six gun on my hip, smelling the whiskey in the wood; and then I could read the whole book! This was the magic Mr. Porter brought to the weekend campfire.

Fed and read, played out and weary, I would crawl into my sleeping bag as the fire burned low, leaving the remainder of the Friday evening to the grownups to do grown up things while I dreamed of Saturday morning adventures.

Most Saturday mornings we bobbed about in York Harbor at daybreak terrorizing flounder. Fish aboard; boat hoisted onto the roof of our car, we returned to a hearty breakfast, quick change into swim trunks and a full day on the beach. But this Saturday morning it was raining. A deep, impenetrable Atlantic fog smothered the coastline, whispering right up against our trailer, obscuring the landscape, cancelling the fishing trip, but not the hearty breakfast.

As we munched a Wheaties breakfast and made alternate plans for the day, my Dad said he wanted to have a talk with me. Usually this meant I was in some kind of trouble, but I was pretty sure my slate was clean, except for the moping.

"C'mon", he said when we finished eating, "Let's go for a little walk."

The steady rain of early morning had lightened to a faint drizzle so walk we did, just the two of us, along Long Sands Beach until we took a seat on the rocks above the waves and my Dad got down to business.

"Is this whole Keith situation still bothering you?" He asked, knowing it was.

---

[6] Gun Fog, William Colt MacDonald.

"Yeah", I replied, "It doesn't seem fair, the way they did it I mean. I passed all my courses."

"You got off on the wrong foot up there. I know you didn't really want to go in the first place, but you didn't behave well while you were there. They had a right to make you leave."

"But...," I began.

"No buts, their school, their rules. Your mother and I probably shouldn't have made you go there in the first place."

"I wanted to try it Dad, but I wanted to leave on my own terms when I found out I didn't like it."

My Dad thought about that for a moment then said, "So basically you're upset because things didn't turn out the way you wanted them to?" I nodded, only beginning to understand.

"Life is going to turn out that way quite a few times, son. You don't have to get used to it, or think it's alright when it does, but you have to know it's going to happen, sooner or later and once or twice again."

We both sat for a minute looking out over the water. Then my father pulled out his wallet and extracted a faded yellow sheet of paper, folded in fours, well-worn with time. He carefully unfolded it.

"I have something for you. I cut this out of a magazine when I was about your age. I didn't get to read a lot when I was growing up, I was always too busy, but this I read, and I kept it with me."

He carefully placed the page on his knee before holding it up to read. "This is by a guy named Kipling, Rudyard Kipling. You heard of him?

"Gunga Din", I answered, "The Jungle Book, The Man Who Would Be King." I could go on. My Dad smiled.

"That's the guy. I haven't read all his stuff but I have read this. I know most of it by heart and I've tried along the way to live up to what he's writing about. I think you'll hear something in it that may help you. This is a poem called "IF", it goes like this...

> *"If you can keep your head when all about you*
> *Are losing theirs and blaming it on you,*
> *If you can trust yourself when all men doubt you,*
> *But make allowance for their doubting too;*
> *If you can wait and not be tired by waiting,*
> *Or, lied about, don't deal in lies,*
> *Or, being hated, don't give in to hating,*
> *And yet don't look too good, nor talk too wise;*
> *If you can dream and not make dreams your master,*
> *If you can think and not make thoughts your aim,*
> *If you can meet with triumph and disaster*
> *And treat those two imposters just the same,"*

I would never forget the sound of my father's voice that day, solid with love and caring, rhapsodized by the crashing of the waves which underlined the import of the words he recited. He continued...

> *"If you can bear to hear the truth you've spoken,*
> *Twisted by knaves to make a trap for fools,*
> *Or watch the things you gave your life to broken,*
> *And stoop and build 'em up with worn out tools.*
>
> *If you can make one heap of all your winnings*
> *And risk it on one game of pitch and toss*
> *And lose, and start again at your beginnings*
> *And never breathe a word about your loss,*
>
> *If you can force your heart and nerve and sinew*
> *To serve your turn long after they are gone,*
> *And so hold on when there is nothing in you,*
> *Except The Will which says to you, "Hold On!"*
>
> *If you can talk with crowds and keep your virtue,*
> *Or walk with kings, nor lose the common touch,*
> *If neither foes nor loving friends can hurt you,*

If all men count with you, but none too much,
If you can fill the unforgiving minute
With sixty seconds worth of distance run,
Yours is the Earth and everything that's in it.
And, which is more, You'll Be A Man My Son".[7]

When he finished he carefully smoothed the page and handed it to me. "This is yours now Son. I hope it helps you along the way." I didn't know what to say. I sat there reading over the words, hearing, as I always would, my Dad's voice speaking the lines. I had passed over these words before in some musty school book, taking note but not notice of what Mr. Kipling was saying but this time the words flowed through my Dad and I knew he was sharing something of value to him with me. A gift of enormous value.

"I don't know if I can do all that stuff, Dad." I said. "Trust yourself when all men doubt you...make allowance for their doubting too...being hated don't give in to hating..."

"There's a lot there," he agreed, "Some of it you just have to grow into. Give yourself a chance, I believe you can do it." And he put his arm around my shoulders and gave me a hug. My moping period was officially over. Somewhere in Mr. Kipling's passage as read by my Father, the weight had been lifted from me. I felt like I had guidelines now that I had not possessed before. And then my Dad added, "Remember son, you can't control how other people are going to treat you. You can control how you treat others, and how you treat yourself."

We walked back to the trailer then and as we did the sun broke through, the fog lifted, the weekend beckoned. By noon I had traded my rain slicker for my bathing suit and I was off to the beach with my family. There was sun and sand, brisk Atlantic breezes, cresting waves and skimming surf. Things felt much better in my world.

That Saturday night after dinner had been served and devoured, after my brothers and their pals had wandered off and my Mom retreated to the bedroom, my Dad, Mr. Porter and I sat around the campfire. Mr.

---

[7] "IF", Rudyard Kipling

Porter had finished yet another paperback and, in his deep and sonorous voice he read…

"And somewhere in there was springtime. The corpse mines were closed down. The soldiers all left to fight the Russians. In the suburbs, the women and children dug rifle pits. Billy and the rest of the group were locked up in the stable in the suburbs. And then, one morning, they got up to discover the door was unlocked. World War Two in Europe was over. Birds were talking.
One bird said to Billy Pilgrim, "Poo-tee-weet?"[8]

Thus ends a novel by Kurt Vonnegut, "Slaughterhouse Five". Mr. Porter read those last paragraphs verbatim and then he told us why.

"Life is full of surprises. Mine sure has been. Not all of the surprises are good, sometimes they don't seem to make any sense at all. What I believe the young man in this book learned is that events in our lives, even the most terrible, will pass if we hang on. And always there will be a little bird around to remind us life goes on."

Sitting around that campfire with my Dad, and Mr. Porter I felt incredibly grown up. Both my father and Mr. Porter had fought in World War Two, so had Mr. Vonnegut. Enduring those most dire circumstances had made them the men they were today. Surviving my miniscule melodramas might do the same for me. I couldn't acknowledge that before.

This weekend, like so many others in The Yorks was exactly what I needed, a respite and a reset, a reminder of who I was and how lucky I was to have the family I had and The Yorks to share with them. Mr. Porter gave me his paperback copy of "Slaughterhouse Five" to take home with me to share with Margaret Mary. My Dad's precious poem was tucked away in my notebook and in my heart. I might not be "Keith Academy Material" but now I finally felt the material that I was, or could develop, with all the help I had around me, was going to be just fine, thank you.

---

[8] Slaughterhouse Five, Kurt Vonnegut.

"The Big Clock", Lowell High School, Lowell, Mass.

Chapter 16

BUTCHIE, NOW KEVIN

"Butchie Martin's after ya!" Teddy was out of breath, as alarmed already as I was growing by the second.

"Why's Butchie after me? I don't even know him?" My question was more about panic than curiosity.

"I don't know," Teddy answered, "did you look at his sister or something?"

"I don't even know what his sister looks like!" Panic plus bewilderment equals terror.

"I don't even wanna' know what his sister looks like." Teddy agreed.

The day had started out pleasantly enough. I was starting my second month at Lowell High, sophomore year fall of 1962. I liked my classes, a couple of my teachers were funny and seemed to really like what they were doing. I liked changing rooms for different subjects, laughing and chatting with friends in the hallways. I liked the lunchroom with long metal tables and a 25 cent hot lunch. I liked wearing a string tie to school and nobody saying anything about it. I also liked seeing a girl named Barbara Mitchell across the hall and getting a funny feeling in my stomach that would later be called love. And now the toughest guy in Lowell is after me and I don't have the slightest idea why.

"How do you know Butchie's after me?" Maybe there was some mistake.

"He's in my shop class. He asked me about you and I told him we were friends. Then he told me to tell my friend to meet him after school, under the clock, today." Teddy spoke as if he were reading my obituary.

Under the clock was Lowell High ground zero. Kids met up there after school for lots of reasons. If you were meeting a girl there that was a good thing, if it was a guy usually not so much. Dates were made under the clock, grudges were settled under the clock, fates, like mine, were determined under the clock.

"You gonna go?" Teddy wanted to know.

Not going really wasn't an option. Big time chickening out, was worse than whatever fate awaited. Besides if Butchie was after me the sooner I found out why the better. I hoped.

"Yeah, I guess so." The only thing I could think of that was worse than having to meet Butchie under the clock was having him looking for me because I wasn't there.

"I'm coming too," Teddy volunteered.

"Thanks, Ted. If a fight starts you can carry me home." And we both laughed, sort of.

The rest of the day dragged by like looming doom, time passed very quickly, then much too slowly. Everything I did I felt like I was doing for the last time. And I still didn't have the slightest idea why Butchie Martin was after me.

3 O'clock was the end of the school day at Lowell High. At 3:08 I was under the clock, with Teddy, waiting for Butchie. I was a little surprised a crowd wasn't gathering. Usually when there was going to be a fight lots of kids showed up to watch the festivities. But the crowd swirled around us taking little notice of Teddy and me. Then Butchie appeared out of the crowd.

Butchie kind of looked like a bag of muscles with a crew cut. He was carrying his school shirt over his shoulder and wearing a t-shirt with no sleeves. His arms bulged like they were full of rocks. Big rocks.

"Hi Ted," he said before turning his attention to me. "You the guy who got kicked out of Keith?"

"That's me," I replied hoping I wasn't about to get kicked out of life.

"Ted, you mind if I talk to your friend alone a minute?" Butchie didn't sound angry or even particularly menacing and Teddy and I exchanged a look as Teddy stepped away, but not too far away.

"I never liked Keith guys very much but Steve Welch says you're an okay guy."

Steve Welch played on the Red Sox with me and Teddy. I gulped waiting for Butchie to continue.

"You know my sister, Beth?"

Here it comes. I was struggling to find the least offensive way of saying no as Butchie continued, "She goes to Keith Hall and she knows this girl named Margaret Mary Sullivan."

So far so good, I couldn't imagine Butchie was going to beat up Margaret Mary.

"Margaret Mary is my friend. She's a really nice person." I answered.

"That's what my sister says too, she says Margaret Mary is the smartest girl in the whole school."

"That's her alright." I was starting to relax, just a little.

"But you're not her boyfriend or anything, right?"

"No, but she's my best friend. Why do you want to know?" I asked as mildly as I could.

"I've seen her a coupl'a times when I went to pick up my sister. You think she'd go out with me if I asked her?"

I was totally at a loss for words. This was the last thing I expected to hear even after spending most of the day wondering what the last thing I was ever going to hear was. Butchie even looked a little nervous as he waited for my answer. I was a little nervous waiting for my answer too.

"I was gonna' ask her to the Harvest Moon dance next weekend." Butchie added.

"I really don't know what she'd say Butch, but I don't think she'd go out with you unless she knew you first."

"That's why I wanted to talk to you," Butch replied, "I thought maybe you could, you know, introduce us or something."

Wow, was all I could think. Life was getting more complicated all the time. I sure didn't want to put Margaret Mary into a bad situation or embarrass her or anything, but I also didn't want to aggravate Butchie by not doing him a favor. Making up my mind quickly I decided Margaret Mary came first.

"I can ask Margaret Mary if she'd like to meet you. She's meeting me after school tomorrow at Brighams. If she says okay I'll tell you and you can come on over if you want."

"Yeah, I could do that." Butchie smiled. "Thanks, man, I appreciate this." And he shook my hand. His fist felt like it was made out of rocks too.

After supper that night I walked over to Margaret Mary's house. This was going to be interesting. As we took our seats on her front porch I decided to get the ball rolling.

"Something happened at school today."

"I certainly hope so," Margaret Mary replied, "that is what we go to school for." Margaret Mary was in one of her deep thinker moods.

"No, I mean something about you happened at school today." That got her attention, deep thinking aside. I continued, "You remember Butchie Martin?"

"I know his sister, Beth. She goes to Keith. She's very nice, but a little shy."

After a summer of deep thought Margaret Mary had decided to give Keith Hall one more year. I hoped she would be coming to Lowell High with me but that was not her decision. So at Keith she remained, with Butchie Martin's sister.

"Well, Butchie's not shy and he kind of seems like a nice guy and he wants to ask you to the Harvest Moon Dance next weekend."

Margaret Mary took a moment or two to think that one over. "And how is it that you know what this Butch person wants to do?"

"I met him after school today, under the clock. He asked me to introduce him to you."

"And you said you would?" Her tone rising in what sounded like a bit of annoyance.

"I said I would ask you. Please don't get mad at me. I didn't know what to do and he was like, alright about the way he asked."

"I'm not upset and you are doing the right thing by asking." Margaret Mary's voice was returning to friendly. "Why don't you ask Butch to meet us at Brigham's after school tomorrow? You can introduce us and then leave us alone for a while but wait for me and we can take the bus home together. Will you do that?"

Of course I would and I did. Now I was watching Margaret Mary and Butchie sitting in a booth at Brighams getting to know one another. I hoped this would turn out well.

And apparently it had. Afterward when Margaret Mary met Teddy and I at the bus stop she was all smiles.

"So, how'd it go?" I asked, Teddy hovering at my shoulder.

"Kevin is very nice. He is going to take me to the Harvest Moon Dance next weekend."

"Wow!" Teddy exclaimed, "You renamed him?"

"Kevin is his real name. He only uses Butchie for his boxing. He actually does not like being called Butchie when he's not boxing." Margaret Mary explained.

You can bet I was going to keep that in mind.

"So what did you guys talk about?" I asked.

Once again Margaret Mary's patience and understanding shone through.

"Personal things." She offered, "But Kevin did ask about you and Teddy. I told him you were both very important to me. And he told me how important his sister Beth is to him." But we already knew that.

Satisfied that so far this escapade had gone well we rode the bus home and every now and then Teddy would chuckle and mutter under his breath, "Kevin".

The next day I was not surprised when Butchie, now Kevin, sought us out at lunchtime. Me and Teddy were sitting at an end table when he came over.

"Hi guys," he said as approached our table. "Mind if I join you?"

Yeah, right, like we'd say so if we minded, but Butchie was being friendly, smiling at me and Ted. We nodded, he sat down.

"Will you guys tell me a little bit about Maggie?" He asked, "She seems really nice."

"She lets you call her Maggie?" Teddy sounded surprised.
"Yeah, isn't that what you call her?"

Yes for Ted, no for me, she would always be Margaret Mary in my book of time, but we both kind of nodded as he continued, "She calls me Kevin, which is my real name. You guys can call me Kevin too, if you want." We wanted and relaxed just a little more in his company.

"Whadd'ya want to know about Maggie?" Teddy asked.

"You know, what does she like, what makes her happy, things like that." Butchie, now Kevin spoke in earnest and I was really impressed that these things were important to him.

"She's a really good dancer," Teddy offered, nudging me in the side, "unlike some other people I know." I let that one go, the less said about my dancing the better.

"She likes books, all kinds of books and the truth, you should always tell Margaret Mary the truth, you can't fool her about that." I contributed.

"Books, huh?" I'm not much of a book guy." Butchie now Kevin admitted.

"Well, stick to the truth then," I added, "but a book or two wouldn't hurt."

"She likes Elvis a lot, and Brenda Lee." Teddy added.

"Yeah? I like Elvis, Brenda Lee's alright too." He said.

"You're still gonna' need a book." I cautioned.

"Maybe you could, like, help me pick out a book, something she would like."

It was amazing how fast life was changing, yesterday I was worried this guy was going to pound me, today he's asking me to pick him out a book.

"I'm meeting Maggie at Brighhams on Friday. I could talk to her about it."

I agreed to get him a book and there was absolutely no question about which book. We finished our lunches and I told Butchie, now Kevin I'd meet him after school, under the clock, with a book. The strangeness went on and on.

"Huckleberry Finn?" He said, holding the dog eared paperback I handed him. "I think we were supposed to read this last year or something. Is this the one where the guy tricks all the other kids into painting a fence for him? I kind of liked that one."

"No, but you're close. That was Tom Sawyer. Same guy wrote this one, Mark Twain, he's my favorite author, Margaret Mary likes him a lot too. Huckleberry Finn is Tom Sawyer's best friend."

"So what's this one about?" He asked turning the book over in his hands.

This is something I had thought a lot about, talked through with Margaret Mary and listened carefully to Sean about.

"Freedom," I answered, "and living by your own rules as long as they don't hurt anyone else. It's about doing the right thing even if everyone else thinks it's wrong and it's about a really cool trip down the Mississippi River on a raft."

"Sounds good," Butchie, now Kevin said, holding my favorite book with a new reverence.

"If you like it you can keep it." I offered, continuing a life-long habit of giving books to my friends.

"Thanks," He replied. "I gotta go meet my sister. Maybe we can talk about this before I see Maggie."

A two day read of Huckleberry Finn, this guy meant business. I waved as we went our separate ways from under the clock.

We didn't see Butchie, now Kevin for the next two days. Me and Teddy ate our lunches at the same metal table and twice I almost went over and asked Barbara Mitchell if she'd go with me to the Harvest

Moon Dance, but I chickened out. Then on Friday afternoon he came over to our table holding his copy of Huckleberry Finn. He looked troubled.

"So what did you think?" I asked after the hellos as he took a seat with us.

"I didn't like it very much", Kevin admitted, "I stopped reading it because of all the nigger talk."

Feeling a bit of alarm I asked, "What do you mean, I don't understand."

He looked me straight in the eye and replied, "I train with a lot of colored guys down at the gym. Most of them are good guys, they're my friends. I don't like hearing them called niggers, at the gym or in a book."

Wow, again, was all I could think. Wow was getting to be a daily experience for me. Teddy was being appropriately silent.

"I agree with you Kevin," I began, "I don't think colored people should be called niggers either. It's what Margaret Mary calls a filthy expression."

"Then how come you two like this book so much?"

Gathering my thoughts carefully and assembling all the insights I had gained from long conversations and consideration of Mark Twain's writing, I began, "Mark Twain is writing about how things were when he was growing up in Missouri over a hundred years ago. People were different then, people talked different then. Huckleberry Finn is growing up in a world where slavery was still legal and his neighbors and friends thought it was alright to own colored people like they were cattle or property. Calling a colored person nigger back then was as common as trash. I'm not saying it was right and I don't believe Mark Twain was either but you couldn't write about those times without using the language people spoke in those times."

Butchie, now Kevin, listened attentively, turning the book over and over on the tabletop.

"Did you read the whole book?" I asked.

"Nah, only up to where he meets Jim on the island and is thinking of turning him in to the slave catchers."

"Okay," I said reaching for the book. "Can I read you just one part that happens a little later? This is when Huckleberry finally decides he is going to turn Jim in and writes a letter to Miss Watson who owned Jim before he ran off."

He pushed the book toward me nodding his head. I turned the familiar pages quickly and began:

I felt good and all washed clean of sin for the first time. I had never felt so in my life, and I knowed I could pray now. But I didn't do it straight off, but laid the paper down and set there thinking – thinking how good it was all this happened so, and how near I come to being lost and going to hell. And went on thinking. And got to thinking over our trip down the river; and I see Jim before me all the time: in the day, and in the night time, sometimes moonlight, sometimes storms, and we a-floating along, talking and singing and laughing. But somehow I couldn't seem to strike no places to harden me against him, but only the other kind. I'd see him standing my watch on top o' his 'n, 'stead of calling me, so I could go on sleeping; and see him how glad he was when I came back out of the fog; and when I came to him again in the swamp, up there where the feud was; and such like times; and would always call me honey, and pet me, and do everything he could think of for me, and how good he always was; and at last I struck the time I saved him by telling the men we had smallpox aboard, and he was so grateful, and said I was the best friend old Jim ever had in the world, and the only one he's got now; and then I happened to look around and see that paper.

It was a close place. I took it up, and held it in my hand, I was a-trembling, because I got to decide, forever, betwixt two things, and I knowed it. I studied it a minute, sort of holding my breath, and then I says to myself: "All right then, I'll go to hell" and tore it up.[9]

I loved this book and I loved those words, that decision to do right in spite of the whole world AND GO TO HELL if that was the cost. When I finished reading there was a familiar lump in my throat and once again, unbidden, tears had filled my eyes.

Neither Butchie, now Kevin nor Teddy said anything for a moment. Butchie, now Kevin picked the book up with a renewed reverence and said, "Maybe I should read a little more of this." Teddy nodded his head in agreement as a thought occurred to me. Feeling again that I might be stepping off a cliff I suggested,

"You remember Kevin about what I said about always telling Margaret Mary the truth?"

Kevin nodded. Teddy listened.

"What you said before about not liking to hear colored people called niggers that was the truth, your truth. Maybe books are not your truth and you shouldn't feel like you have to read them to make somebody else, even if it's Margaret Mary, like you."

"I don't like books a lot either," Teddy volunteered, "Unless they're about sports or something."

"You sayin' I shouldn't read books?" Butchie, now Kevin snorted, sounding a little on edge.

"No," I answered quickly, "I'm saying you shouldn't feel like you have to do something that's not you just to make someone like you."

"You mean just be myself, who I really am?"

"All or nothing, as long as it's the truth. If Margaret Mary doesn't like you then that's better than having her like you for being something you're not."

---

[9] The Adventures of Huckleberry Finn, Mark Twain

Butchie, now Kevin stood up and picked up Huckleberry Finn again. "Maybe I'll give this another chance." He said and started to walk away, then he stopped and said, "This better work." And smiled, I was very glad he smiled.

After he left I thought very carefully about what I had said. Then I took a deep breath, walked across the lunchroom to where Barbara Mitchell was sitting with her friends and asked her to the Harvest Moon Dance. She said yes.

Chapter 17

THE END OF THE WORLD

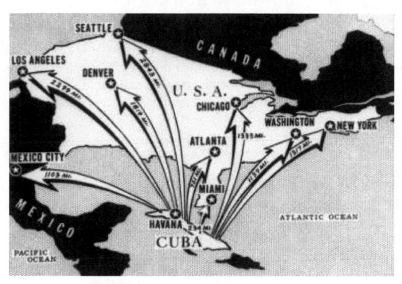

Front Page Newspaper Illustration,
Cuban Missile Strike Targets,
October, 1962

The Harvest Moon Dance was on a Friday night. I went with Barbara
Mitchell, Margaret Mary and Kevin made their social debut, to much
whispering, and Teddy came with Linda Rogers. We all sat together
at a table with a pumpkin in the middle and had a wonderful time. We
danced, yes I danced, to the music of Neil Sedaka, Connie Francis,
Ray Charles and Shelly Fabares among many others. The general
consensus was that Butchie, now Kevin, was as awkward and self-
conscious a dancer as I was, though nobody was going to tell him that,
and when he and I got up and fake danced together to Gene Pitney
warbling, "Only Love Can Break A Heart" the whole room,
EVERYBODY, went dead silent and fled the dance floor until
Margaret Mary, Barbara and Linda rose to their feet clapping like mad
and Teddy started laughing so hard he turned blue.

Exactly three days later we learned the world was about to end, for
real.

The headline of the Lowell Sun screamed on Tuesday, October 23, 1962:

SHOWDOWN HOURS AWAY
U.S. AND RUSSIA HEAD FOR
COLLISION COURSE

Medium and long range Russian nuclear missiles had been discovered in Cuba. They were secretly sent there and armed by Soviet Russia and posed, according to White House analysts, an immediate threat to the entire United States.

That night Walter Cronkite warned of approaching nuclear doomsday on the CBS Evening News while Chet Huntley and David Brinkley grimly reported the mushrooming specter of imminent Atomic War on NBC and John Daley rang a similar death knell on ABC.

NORAD had gone to DEFCOM 3, which in plain English meant that nuclear bombs had been armed and loaded aboard our B-52 bombers and were standing by to strike strategic targets in the Soviet Union if so ordered.

Preparations were also underway for surgical airstrikes on the missile sites in Cuba followed by a full scale military invasion of the island. And that evening President Kennedy preempted all three major networks to inform the nation about what would come to be called the Cuban Missile Crisis.

At 7PM a grim and tense President Kennedy addressed the nation. Once again we had gathered in our living room. Mom, Dad and I, my two brothers, along with Sean and Margaret Mary. We were all dead silent as President Kennedy appeared on the screen. Sean poured himself a tumbler of Irish whiskey which he held to his chest as President Kennedy read an ominous sounding prepared statement,

> *"It shall be the policy of this nation to regard any nuclear missile launched from Cuba against any nation in the Western hemisphere as an attack by the Soviet Union on the United States, requiring a full retaliatory response upon the Soviet Union."*

"What's that mean Dad? A retaliatory response?" My brother Bob asked.

"It means if they bomb us we will bomb them back." My Dad replied.

"If they bomb us we may not be able to bomb them back." Sean added.

"Sssh," My Mother hissed, "I want to hear this." She hugged my youngest brother, John, closer to her on the sofa as our President continued,

> "*To halt this offensive build up a strict quarantine on all offensive military equipment under shipment to Cuba is being initiated. All ships of any kind bound for Cuba will, if found to contain cargoes of offensive weapons, be turned back. This quarantine will be extended, if needed, to other types of cargoes and carriers.*"

As the President paused a ghastly silence settled over our living room. After a moment my Dad whispered, "This could start a war."

"This almost certainly will start a war." Sean said, placing a protective hand on Margaret Mary's shoulder and gulping a large swallow of his drink.

When the President's speech ended and the gloomy network commentary began there was a knock on our front door. It was Teddy, come over from next door, and looking frightened. As my Mom let him in we heard the roar of his Brother Chris' motorcycle speed away.

"Can I stay over here with you guys for a while?" Teddy asked, "Connie's crying and Chris got real mad and my father's not home yet and I don't know what's goin' on."

My Mom brought Teddy into the living room where he sat on the floor next to me and my brother, Bob.

"Were you guys watching TV?" I asked.

"Yeah, Chris said like, "This is it", and punched a wall and Connie is trying to call my Dad and I didn't know what to do."

"I don't think any of us know what to do Teddy." My Mother offered. Margaret Mary was strangely silent through all this and all I could feel was that something bad, really bad, was about to happen.

"What do you think Mr. Ferrier?" Sean asked after taking another large swallow of his Tullamore Dew.

"I think our President has his finger on a trigger he may be forced to pull."

And ever so slightly I heard Margaret Mary choke back a sob and saw my Mother pull my brother yet closer to her.

As Walter Cronkite continued to expound on the number and nature of naval ships making up the blockade and how many bombers were being readied at airfields all over the country, churches all around Lowell and all over the country threw open their doors for prayer vigils, special Masses were offered, long lines formed at confessionals and pleas for peace offered.

"Are you gonna' have to go back in the Army Dad?" My brother John asked.

"No, this is not going to be that kind of a war, John." He answered.

"What kind of a war is it going to be Mr. Ferrier?" Teddy asked, his voice shaking.

"We don't know that there is going to be any kind of a war at all yet," my Mother interjected. "I'm sure President Kennedy is going to do all he can to keep a war from happening."

"And we should all pray that that will be enough." Sean added, his words slurred by the whiskey.

At that point there was another knock at our front door. It was Connie, Ted's older sister, it was clear she had been crying.

"Is Teddy here?" She asked as my Mom ushered her in.

"Yes, he's with the others in the living room." Mom answered. Teddy got up and went to his sister, putting his arm around her waist.

"Dad called, he's on his way home and he wants us all to stay home till he gets here." Connie said. As she and Teddy made their goodbye's Sean rose shakily to his feet, assisted by Margaret Mary.

"We too shall make our way home. Thank you for sharing the evening with us. Home is where we should all stay close to this night." Margaret Mary left without saying a word but exchanged a long look of caring with my Mother and she nodded quickly to me. She looked like she was fighting back tears as they went out our front door.

We did not put the TV on again for the rest of the evening. My Mom and Dad said we were going to do a "camp in" and sleep in our basement tonight.

So we took up sleeping bags and sofa cushions and went downstairs where I dreamed fitfully of the night sky flashing white and the whole world going up in flames.

The next morning we all awoke a little stiff and tired but thankful we had awoken at all. My Dad immediately put on the TV and the reporter said tense negotiations were underway with the Soviet Union and that we were "eyeball to eyeball" with the Russians but there had been no escalation yet.
Yet.

"There's a 9 O'clock mass this morning at the Immaculate. Get dressed, we're all going to go." My Dad announced as we filled cereal bowls and buttered toast.

"Today's not Sunday", John said, "how come we gotta' go to church?"

"To ask god not to let a war start." My Mother replied.

And once again I had that terrible feeling that something awful was about to happen.

"What about school, Dad?" I managed to ask.

"We're going to stay around the house today." Dad answered. "We'll come right home after church."

"Can I go see if Margaret Mary and Sean want to come with us?" I asked.

"Yes, but come right back."

As I walked slowly over to Margaret Mary's I was frightened by how worried my Mom and Dad looked. That bad, bad feeling was getting stronger.

Margaret Mary met me on her porch stairs and explained that she couldn't go to church with us because Sean wasn't feeling well.

"From the whiskey," she added sadly.

"You goin' to school today?" I asked.

"I'm going to stay here with Sean. Please come over later this afternoon if you can."

"I will." And then we hugged each other, hoping we were not saying goodbye, and I went off to church with my family.

Neither my Mother nor Father went to work that day. My brothers and I did not go to school. My Dad mostly stayed in the living room watching the newscasts of naval ships surrounding Cuba, strategic aircraft being readied for flight, and brief case toting diplomats desperately exchanging messages. That afternoon the Soviet News Agency, TASS, released a telegram from Soviet Premier Khrushchev to President Kennedy warning him that "the United States outright piracy" would lead to war." Not could, would. And the drumbeats grew ever louder.

The headlines for the Lowell Sun on Wednesday, October 24th read:

ARMED SHOWDOWN NEAR
SOVIET SHIPS HEAD FOR CUBA
AS BLOCKADE BEGINS DEFENSE DEPARTMENT
RELEASES PHOTOS OF RED MISSILE SITES

My mother watched us all closely throughout the day, warning us not to stray out of our yard and when I asked if I could go over to Margaret Mary's to see if she was alright she agreed and suggested I invite them to dinner that night. Dinner and more news of the Apocalypse.

When I went outside I saw Teddy standing in his driveway watching the street. Chris had not come home from the night before.

"Hi Ted, wanna' come over to Margaret Mary's with me? I just want to see if she's alright."

"I can't," Ted answered, "My Dad said not to leave the yard."

I noticed Ted's father's car was in the driveway. "Your Dad's home?"

"Yeah, he's not opening the garage today. I couldn't believe it, he even opened the garage on Christmas. He's really mad that Chris didn't come home last night."

"Do you know where he is?"

"No, I just hope he's OK."

And about then we heard the growl of a motorcycle getting closer. In a moment Chris appeared at the end of the street and cruised into the driveway. The first thing we noticed when he climbed off his bike was a purple shiner and a swollen lip. Chris grunted at Teddy and me as he started into the house.

"Who'd you get in a fight with? " Teddy asked as Chris walked away.

"Some Cuban guy." Chris tossed over his shoulder and went into the house.

Teddy and I looked at each other and shook our heads. Without a word between us I started over to Margaret Mary's and Teddy followed Chris into the house. Margaret Mary was sitting on her front porch reading when I arrived. We sat quietly for a few moments, then Sean joined us. He looked terrible, haggard and shaky. Margaret Mary would not look at him as he took a seat between us.

"David lad, I'm glad you're here. I have come to apologize to my darling daughter and to you as well for my behavior evening last." Margaret Mary still would not look at her father.

"I drank far too much last night and not enough this morning and I should like to tell you both why." Margaret Mary snuck a peek at her father as he continued, "You see as we watched the news last night a terrible, terrible thought occurred to me and that thought was, and is, that if this war shall begin this very day there is nothing, absolutely nothing I can do to protect my precious child from the peril. And because I could not stop thinking that, I drank to stop thinking anything at all. I apologize to you both for this and ask for your forgiveness, my darling daughter and you David and your entire family."

Margaret Mary turned to her father and put her arms around his neck, burying her face in his shoulder. They stayed that way for a few minutes as I sat as quietly as I could. When they separated Sean said, "I believe coffee, dark and strong, would serve me well. If you two would excuse me I shall repair to the scullery." Wherever that was.

When Margaret Mary and I were alone I asked, "Have you heard from Kevin?"

"He's at his grandmother's with Beth. Both his parents had to work today and they didn't want her to be alone." Margaret Mary explained. "David, what do you think is going to happen?"

It frightened me to even consider the possible answers to that question. We had all seen the movies and TV shows about atomic bombs and how they could destroy entire cities with one blast. The newspapers said that Russia had just as many atomic bombs as we did and if we ever fought them nobody could win, everybody would die. I knew Margaret Mary knew all this as well as I so I tried to think of an answer that wasn't horrible.

"President Kennedy will think of something, he's the smartest guy we know. He doesn't want a war, I just hope the Russians don't want one either."

"Why would anyone want a war that would destroy the whole world?" Margaret Mary asked.

A question I could not answer and wondered if anyone could.

"I should go and see if my father is alright." She added. Then we hugged again, hoping once more that it was not for the last time. As I walked back to my house I remembered that I had forgotten to ask them to dinner.

We slept in the basement again that evening but on Thursday my Dad and Mom had to go back to work and we had to go to school. The day passed, sometime feeling almost normal, until we learned that night that our Navy had begun stopping ships headed to Cuba. In the first glimmer of good news all week the networks reported that fourteen Russian ships in route to Cuba had turned back before encountering the blockade. A flicker of optimism crept into the newscasts.

The Lowell Sun headline for Thursday, October 25, 1962 read:

DIVERSION OF SOME SOVIET SHIPS STALLS US RUSSIA SHOWDOWN

My Mother announced that we would all sleep in our upstairs beds that night and as clandestine diplomats scurried between embassy's and offices things took a turn for the much, much worse.

The Lowell Sun headline for Friday, October 26, 1962 read:

US STOPS, BOARDS SOVIET SHIP INTERCEPT CARRIED OUT BY BOARDING PARTIES

Despite this escalation tensions initially seemed to lessen. Messrs. Huntley and Brinkley, Cronkite and Daley sounded more reassuring as they tracked negotiations between the White House and the Kremlin. No shots had been fired thus far.

On Friday night The Flintstones returned to the air along with Sunset Strip and Rawhide. The networks resumed their campaign to remind us we should be eating Sugar Pops and Hostess Cupcakes, filling our gas tanks with Texaco and smoking Kent Cigarettes with the Micronite Filter. Whatever that was.

On Saturday morning Teddy and I negotiated a trip to Shedd Park by promising to return home immediately if we heard air raid sirens. Such was the state of affairs even as forebodings eased and life tried to sneak back to normal. We stopped by Margaret Mary's house where Sean told us she had gone by taxi to Kevin's grandmother's house across town but that she promised to be home by suppertime. Sean joked that it was at last looking like we all may have a home by suppertime. Teddy and I thought that was funny. Sort of.

Nobody from our gang was there when Teddy and I got to Shedd Park.

Parents were still keeping their families close by, just in case. Barbara Mitchell and her family had driven up to Sebago Lake in Maine where they had a cabin in the woods. Safer, her father thought. Teddy said Linda Rogers and her family were going to a Novena at the Immaculate that afternoon and that they had gone to church every day this week to pray. Somehow that almost sounded normal.

Teddy and I hung out at the park for a couple of hours without seeing any of our friends. Teddy told me that his father and Chris had had a big fight about his not coming home that night and about the fight that Chris had gotten into. Chris threatened to move out and his father said go ahead, but nothing happened. Teddy said Chris and his father had arguments all the time and that Connie usually got them to make peace for a while. Teddy said his father growled it didn't make any difference anyway since the whole damned world was about to blow up. I sure hoped Teddy's father was wrong.

The headlines for the Lowell Sun that Saturday evening proclaimed:

JFK REJECTS K PROPOSAL K OFFERS TO SWAP CUBA FOR TURKEY DEMAND CUBAN ROCKET SITES BE DISMANTLED

And the Sunday morning paper read:

US CALL 14,000 A.F. RESERVES ACTS AFTER CUBA OPENS FIRE ON MILITARY PLANES

We attended Mass as a family that morning. From the pulpit Father Murphy asked us all to pray for peace as well as wisdom for our government leaders. An afternoon vigil would be held at the church for more prayer.

Sean and Margaret Mary spent the afternoon at our house as ominous news bulletins interrupted normal television programming. Amidst the drumbeats rumors began to emerge of a deal. Russia would remove its missiles from Cuba if we would remove our missiles from Turkey. We had missiles in Turkey? Sean had been doing some research.

"Throughout the Cold War the United States has been building up its missile presence in Europe. Apparently we have launch sites of our own in Turkey right on the Russian border. Some believe it is the

presence of these missile sites and other sites like them that prompted
Russia to place their missiles in Cuba in the first place."
"So if we give up our sites the Russians will give up theirs?" My Dad
asked.

"Apparently that is the offer." Sean said.

"Pray to God that will happen." My Mother added.

And it did. After another tense round of negotiations, without gunfire,
Russia agreed to begin dismantling the Cuban missile sites. No
Russian warships challenged our blockade and the lingering threat of
nuclear war finally lessened.

On Friday, November 2, 1962 the headline of the Lowell Sun read:

RUSSIANS DISMANTLING BASES

And on Sunday, November 4, 1962 the Lowell Sun reported:

REPORTS SATISFACTORY PROGRESS IN CUBAN MISSILE CRISIS

And finally, in a press conference held at the State Department
Auditorium in Washington, D.C. on November 21, 1962, President
Kennedy announced:

*"I have been today informed by Chairman Khrushchev that all of the
IL-28 bombers now in Cuba will be withdrawn within 30 days. He
also agrees that these planes can be observed and counted as they
leave. Inasmuch as this goes a long way towards reducing the danger
which faced this Hemisphere four weeks ago, I have this afternoon
instructed the Secretary of Defense to lift our naval quarantine.
May I add this final thought? In this week of Thanksgiving there is
much for which we can be grateful as we look back to where we stood
only four weeks ago – the unity of this Hemisphere, the support of our
allies, and the calm determination of the American people. These
qualities may be tested many more times in this decade, but we have
an increased reason to be confident that those qualities will continue
to serve the cause of freedom with distinction in the years to come."*

As I heard these words that Tuesday afternoon I could not recall "calm
determination" or any "increased reason to be confident". I recalled
only sleeping fitfully in the basement of our home, huddled on sofa

cushions and dreaming of the sky catching fire. I recalled Sean slurring his words and shuffling out of our living room, Teddy's sister, Connie, crying and my Mother holding tight to my brother John as we sat together in our living room. I remembered solemn weekday Masses and Chris' black eye, and saying goodbye to Margaret Mary on her front porch and not knowing if I ever would see her again.

As Thanksgiving turned to Christmas that year much was written and said of how we had "won" the Cuban Missile Crisis. Yet what I could recall most was what I had lost. While I realized that we may now be safe from missiles in Cuba, the people who had put them there were still out there. As we presumably unloaded all the nuclear bombs from our own planes I knew they were not being dismantled, but stored, being made ready for the next crisis, the one the President had just told us we would face "many more times" in the coming decade. I had lost the feeling of safety in my own home, in my hometown, in my country. And there was one more thing I had lost, smothered now under the layers of dread I had lived with for the past month. I lost the magic of something very important that happened the night of the Harvest Moon dance.

When the dance ended our whole group walked home together in the silvery October moonlight. Laughing and happy we talked about how Kevin and I's dance was going to be the toast of the schoolyard on Monday, along with Teddy's super version of The Twist. We talked about our favorite records and TV shows and what our plans were for the upcoming Holiday season. Thanksgiving and Christmas were right around the corner and we all agreed a giant stuffed Turkey was our favorite holiday feast.

When we got to High Street I split off from the group to walk Barbara to her front door. We held hands as we walked and didn't talk a lot, shuffling along, scattering the fallen autumn leaves blanketing the sidewalk. When we got to Barbara's house, under her front porch light, I kissed her. My very first, at last, and as dizzying and wonderful and magical as that first kiss was, I could hardly remember it now, faded behind my nightmare of the sky flashing white and the whole world going up in flames.

Death From Above, Oct. 1962

"Sometimes you will never know the value of a moment until it becomes a memory."

Dr. Seuss

Chapter 18

"WE'RE GONNA' WHAT?" REDUX

"We're gonna' learn to what?"

This was a dumber idea than dancing. A lot dumber.

"We're gonna' learn to box", Teddy explained, "Butchie's gonna' teach us."

"Why would we want to learn to box? And I thought we called him Kevin."

"It's Butchie at the gym and that's where we're gonna learn to box." Teddy was happy to announce.

Teddy is my buddy and usually if he has an idea I'll go along with it, but this I did not understand.

"OK, but what about the why part?" Teddy was not an aggressive guy, and neither was I. Boxing was, I thought, for scrappers. I didn't want to scrap.

"Chris says it will toughen me up some," Teddy explained, "He says it can't hurt to know how to defend myself."

Which made sense, at least partial sense, maybe, and I thought the dancing idea was dumb at first and that actually worked out pretty well. Also it was February, 1963, in Lowell, which meant cold and icy and slushy with little to do except stay indoors and wait for spring. Boxing was indoors.

Also Valentine's Day was going to be a little empty for me as Barbara Mitchell's father made her break up with me. She told me her father said he "didn't want his daughter going out with some kid who got thrown out of Keith." Barbara didn't want to disobey her parents any more than I wanted to disobey mine, so we broke up. Just like in an

171

Everly Brothers song. I had to start working on a new reputation. Maybe boxing would help.

"You are going to learn to do what?" Margaret Mary exclaimed that afternoon as we sat on her front porch.

So I told her, and the reasons why and who was going to teach us.

"Kevin did not tell me about this." She said.

"Maybe he didn't feel like he had to." I offered.

"You could get hurt." She added.

"I could get hurt worse if I don't know how to box."

"Fight you mean," Margaret Mary was sounding protective and a little annoyed.

"I've only been in one fight in my whole life," I said, "it lasted about thirty seconds and I got a black eye."

"And your point is?" Margaret Mary had passed protective and amped up the annoyed.

"Well, if I had known how to fight better I might not have gotten the shiner."

"And if you had not gotten the shiner you might not have learned to avoid fighting whenever you can." Margaret Mary had a point there. I didn't like fighting, I didn't like the anger and fear that went with it. I didn't like the confrontation, the ugliness of it, unless there was no other choice. Then I figured it was best to know what I was doing, so off to the gym I was going, after I talked this over with my parents. Margaret Mary grew silent then, perhaps recalling Sean's advice about the "boyos and their sporting".

Sighing she said, "Well just be very careful. I am going to speak to Kevin about this."

"Please don't," I asked, "Kevin is doing Teddy and me a favor by teaching us. This is between him and us, you shouldn't interfere."

Margaret Mary huffed and puffed for just a moment, then agreed. We had always been very honest with one another and that was how I felt. She decided to respect that.

After dinner that night I brought up the boxing idea to my Mom and Dad.

Mom looked at Dad, Dad looked at me, and asked, "What brought this on?" So I told him that initially it was Teddy's idea but I kinda' wanted to too.

My Mom asked if I was being threatened by someone and didn't feel safe. So I told them that wasn't the case either. I just wanted to try it, see what it was like and go with Teddy while he tried it as well. I explained I didn't want to learn so much how to fight other people but how to protect myself if someone wanted to fight me. Eventually promises were made, limits established and permission was given. I was going to learn how to box, I hoped.

That Saturday morning my Dad drove Teddy and me down to Nelson's Gym where Butchie trained. Nelson's was in the rougher part of Lowell, an area of closed down textile mills, one door liquor stores with iron bars across the windows with an abandoned car or two cluttering the street and groups of scruffy looking guys hanging on street corners drinking from brown bottles wrapped tight in brown paper bags and smoking cigarettes.

"Want me to come in with you?" My Dad offered.

"No, Dad. It'll make us look like little kids."

"Okay," he said, "I'll be back at 12:30. We can go over to the Elliot and get a hot dog."

Big smiles from me and Teddy as my Dad drove away. Alone in the parking lot we headed for the door.

The gym was in the corner of an old mill, refurbished for boxing. It had a green metal door and bars on all the windows. Three cracked and moldering cement stairs led up to the landing where the door was. I followed Teddy up the stairs as he took a deep breath and pushed the door open.

You know that minute in the Western movies when the good guy, or the bad guy, walks into the saloon and everybody stops what they're doing and stares at them. That was me and Teddy when we walked into Nelson's. Nobody moved, especially me and Teddy. The silence was very loud until Butchie appeared from the back of the gym. I couldn't have been any more relieved if Davy Crockett, King of the Wild Frontier had showed up to greet us.

"You guys made it, huh?" Butchie offered.

We both gulped and swallowed and nodded our heads. Butchie laughed and said, "Relax, nobody is going to kill you...yet. C'mon, I'll show you where to change."

Which led to our first lesson in training at Nelson's Gym. Nelson's Gym wasn't heated, or barely heated, but mostly not heated at all. It was like, 14 degrees outside, inside maybe 15 degrees. Teddy and I had brought our gym shorts and t-shirts from Lowell High.

"You guys are gonna' freeze to death in those outfits." Butchie laughed. "C'mon, you're gonna' need to move around a little bit."

So we followed Butchie out onto the gym floor. There were two boxing rings side by side in the center of the room, raised from the floor about three feet with aged, multi-stained canvas on the floor, worn but serviceable ring ropes about the edges and bright fluorescent lighting above. The light looked warm, some of the stains looked like blood. Nobody was boxing in either ring. It was freezing out there.

There were about fifteen guys in the gym. None of them looked familiar. In one corner a guy was shadow boxing, light on his feet and lightning fast with his hands, in another a fighter punched into the raised palms of an older guy who was chewing on an unlit cigar. Around the rest of the gym floor fighters jabbed and skipped rope, pounded heavy bags dangling from ceiling chains and rat-a-tatted speed bags with consummate skill.

Everyone looked focused, intent on what they were doing, there was very little chatter or joking around. Boxing, apparently was serious stuff. Several of the fighters nodded at Butchie as we came out, for Teddy and me there were curious glances, sly grins but no sense of animosity. Scary as the place may have looked when we walked in, once we were in, and under Butchie's wing, everybody just went about their business, though it felt like they were watching us from the corner of their eyes.

There were, as I counted carefully, six colored guys in the gym. Swathed as they were in sweat pants and hoodies only an ebony or coffee colored face peeked out from under their headgear. Mostly they ignored us, but I was acutely aware of them.

I had never been around many (any) colored people before. Lowell at the time was largely made up of Greeks and Irish, French and Portuguese and a scattering of other miscellaneous Caucasians. In my eight years at the Immaculate School there were none, zero, people of color, at Keith Academy, none as well. My sophomore class at Lowell High School had just shy of a thousand students. Two were colored, a brother and sister, Lester Brown and Charlene Brown. I had never spoken to either one. I didn't try not to, I just didn't know them, who they were or what they were like. Lester played in the school band, trumpet, I think. He didn't play any sports that I knew of and I had no idea where he lived. Charlene was in my study hall. She sat way over on the other side of the room and seemed to be very quiet. I never saw anyone act any differently toward either of them than to anyone else in the school and it never occurred to me that they would be treated any differently. But somehow they were different, a breed apart, unfamiliar to me and Teddy as well, and undeniably intimidating, I'm not sure why.

The six colored guys at Nelson's were the most I had been around in my life. They looked tough and hard to me and what appeared to be surliness on their part was probably reserve and bitter experience on their part but those were not factors immediately knowable to a slightly frightened, mostly intimidated, and thirteen year old like me. I did know that this was something to talk about later with Margaret Mary, if I got out of this place alive.

"How many sit ups can you guys do?" Butchie asked as we arrived at a corner canvas mat.

"Like 50 maybe," Teddy answered. I nodded in agreement.

"Show me." Butchie said, "Dave, hold Teddy's ankles. Knees up, twist from side to side on the upswing, left elbow, right knee, right elbow, left knee." Butchie stepped back to watch, Teddy hit the floor and I anchored his ankles.

Teddy ran out of gas at 35 sit ups. His face was tomato red when he stopped.

"Your turn," Butchie said, meaning me.

30 sit ups later I was done. Both Teddy and I were in decent shape, baseball shape anyway. I thought I could do more sit ups, so did Teddy.

"Let's try some push-ups," Butchie said, "Fifty." Teddy got 27, I got 31. Butchie shook his head.

"Before either one of you get into the ring you have to be able to do 100 sit ups and 100 push-ups, or else you're gonna get hurt. Start today, four sets of 25 sit ups, five sets of 20 push-ups. That's just to warm up, we'll get to the hard stuff later."

Then he walked away leaving Teddy and me alone in the corner. I could feel eyes on us. Teddy got on the floor, I held his ankles, and he held mine. 25, rest, 20 rest. Three more times. My arms felt like rubber bands. My stomach was one big, sore knot. We weren't cold anymore.

As Teddy and I stood huffing and puffing in our corner Butchie came back along with the older guy who was still chewing his cigar.

"Max", Butchie began, "these are my friends, Dave Ferrier and Teddy Gianoulous. They want to learn how to box."

Max owned Nelson's Gym. His last name was Ginsburg. Go figure. Anyway, Max was a spry and lively older guy, who before World War II was a New England Golden Gloves Champion. There were faded pictures of Max in fighting trim on the wall in his office along with long ago, tarnished trophies and a Golden Gloves Champion Belt, 1939. We would come to learn that Max was ready to turn pro about the time of the attack on Pearl Harbor. He joined the Navy the very next day and spent the next four years in the Pacific. He was aboard the USS Missouri when Japan surrendered on September 2, 1945. He remained in the Navy, boxing throughout the fleet, until his discharge in 1956 after twenty five years of service. He bought Nelson's Gym the following year.

"You the guy who got kicked out of Keith?" Max asked.

Unbelievable. I should wear a sign.

"Costs five bucks a month to train here. Come as often as you want. If you can't pay we can work something out for you to do around here maybe. First rule in my gym," Max continued, "No fighting. We box here. You want to fight do it outside and don't come back in after you do it. You get it?"

We got it, along with the rest of the house rules, of which there were many. No smoking, no alcohol, no swearing, Max didn't like swearing, and spit only in the buckets.

"C'mon, I'll show you how to tape up." Max said as we followed him across the gym floor. Butchie left again, and began hammering on a heavy bag. Loud hammering.

"This is the first thing you do when you come into my gym," Max said, tossing Teddy and I two rolls of Ace bandages to bind our hands. "Those are a buck each, you can pay me later." He added.

Max showed us how to tape our hands, suggested heavy sweats and a hoodie and two pairs of socks. The floor, he explained, gets frosty.

"Do your warm ups first, sit ups and push-ups. Either of you guys know how to jump rope?"

Two no's later we were being shown how.

"Builds up your legs, develops timing, and keeps you from freezing to death in here. Three minutes, rest, three minutes, three times. Got it?" We got it.

"Okay," Max said, "Now I'm going to teach you how to stand." Which I thought I knew how to do. I was wrong.

"See that strip of tape on the floor?" Max asked, "I want you to stand with the line down the middle of your body. Now turn to your side. Put your front toe and back heel on the line, like this." Max turned me, then Teddy so that we were aligned with the tape. "Now keep your feet a little wider than shoulder length apart. Relax, don't forget to breathe, hands up, elbows in, chin down. Now you got it, you're standin'. Boxing is about staying that way."

I looked at Teddy, he had that grin that would have killed him a bear, so did I.

"Now do your rope work, then get dressed so you don't catch pneumonia. Dress warmer next time, if there's gonna' be a next time." Max wandered off, stopping to talk to a group of fighters who stole quick, amused glances at me and Teddy.

We were taking turns with the jump rope, getting better as we went along when Butchie came over.

"How you guys doin' so far? You ready to get in the ring with me?" Butchie was smiling. I hoped he was kidding.

"Uh", Teddy began, "Max told us to get dressed after we finished jumping rope."

That got a big laugh from Butchie. "I know he did. It'll be a while before you guys are ready to get in the ring with anybody. Don't sweat it. You're doing good for your first day." Liked hearing that.

"Do you come here every day, Butch?" Teddy asked.
"Three days a week, sometimes four. But I do my roadwork every day. Five miles. You guys should start running too. Work your way up from a mile, take it slow."

"I don't think I can come here three times a week Butch," I said, "School work plus I don't have a ride." Teddy nodded in agreement, about the ride, he wasn't all that worried about the schoolwork.

"If you wanna' learn how to do this you gotta' work hard. Gettin' in shape is only the first part. You need to be here to learn how. Two days minimum, running every day. Keep up the push-ups and sit ups, you can do those at home. Same with the jump rope. It's up to you." Max came over and joined us about then.

"So, you guys comin' back?"

Teddy and I both said yeah, you bet, and meant it.

"Don't be a coupla' jamokes." He added, "See you next week. Dress warmer." Then he left.

"Hey Butchie," Ted asked, "What's a jamoke?"

"A jamoke is a guy who thinks he wants to do somethin' till he finds out how hard it is, then he don't want to do it anymore." Butchie explained, then turned to go. "I'll see you guys at school Monday."

When Teddy and I were dressed and waiting outside for my Dad I asked, "So what do you think Ted? We gonna do this?"

Teddy looked at me just as my Dad pulled into the parking lot. "Yeah, you think I wanna' be a jamoke?"

So me and Teddy went into training to become boxers. We came back to Nelson's on Wednesday, after school. We brought sweat pants and sweat shirts, sweat socks and beanie caps along with a dollar each for the hand wraps. We walked over from school together, briskly through the rougher parts of town and past the clusters of guys on the street corners. Butchie met us at the gym, he went up to Keith Hall after school to meet his sister and walk her home. Then he jogged over to the gym. Four miles. Each way. Me and Teddy were still working our way up to that.

Nobody paid us much attention when we came in this time. There were about the same number of guys in there, going about their business. Teddy and I changed into our sweats, wrapped our hands and went to our corner for sit ups and push-ups. Max came out of his office and looked around, nodded at Teddy and me and went over to work with a fighter on the speed bag. A few minutes later Butchie came in. When he stashed his jacket and gloves he came over to where Teddy and I were finishing our push-ups.

"How many?" He asked.

"60," I said. Two more sets of twenty. Same for the sit ups, two more sets."

"Good," he answered, "when you're done with those, do your rope work then meet me over at the heavy bag. I'll show you how to punch."

Teddy grinned at me, I grinned back. We were going to learn how to punch.

Max joined us at the bag with Butchie.

"Remember how I told you to stand? Show me." Max took a step back, Teddy and I went into our brand new fighter stance. Max grunted something to Butchie. He turned my shoulders just slightly and Butchie raised Teddy's hands more in front of his face. When they were satisfied with us both Max said, "OK this is your starting position. You want to be a little less than arm's length to the bag. You want to hit the bag without leaning forward too much. Tighten your fist when you punch, loosen it when you snap back. Got it?" Most of it.

"Dave you're up. Throw three punches, left, right, left. Hit with your shoulders and your legs. Exhale when you punch, inhale when you recover."

And I was off. First thing I noticed was how hard the heavy bag was. When I hit it the shock ran all the way up my arm to my shoulder. I quickly threw two more, left, right and stepped back, satisfied, with a huge grin covering my face. Butchie and Max exchanged a look.

"Round one to the bag." Max declared.

I was crushed, but Butchie threw his arm around my shoulder and said, "Relax, he always says that. You're up Teddy."

Teddy ambled up to the bag, set himself and threw three crunchers, right, left, right."

"Southpaws", muttered Max, "Gotta do everythin' backwards."
Max wandered away, leaving us in Butchie's care. I couldn't wait for my turn.

"OK", Butch said, "One guy holds the bag, one guy punches the bag. Three shots, three times then switch. Don't try to break the bag, keep your feet flat on the ground, punch straight, don't forget to breathe. Got it?"

We got it. For the next half hour we pounded and punched, feeling the burn in our arms, in our lungs, the fatigue setting into our legs. I liked the crisp snap of contact, the rhythm of the punches, and the thud on the bag. The more I did it, the more I liked it. Finally Teddy and I stepped back and exchanged a now familiar smile of satisfaction, we were sweating in a very cold room.

It felt terrific.

And so it went on for the next three weeks. Teddy and I spent every Saturday morning till noon and three hours on Wednesday after school learning to punch, counterpunch, duck and cover, step and drag, bob and weave, all in front of the heavy bag, never yet in the ring. Then Butchie told us we were ready.

"How about trying a few rounds? You guys game?" Butchie asked.

Teddy and I, undefeated and unscarred with the heavy bag, were ready. So we thought.

Butchie called over one of the guys, a lightweight, and asked if he wanted to spar a bit with the new guys.

The fighter's name was Antoine Davis, one of the colored boxers I had eyed, but never spoken with at the gym. Antoine had a great smile, when he smiled, and a great sense of humor when he thought something was funny. Sparring with me and Teddy struck him both ways. Butchie made the introductions, Antoine didn't say much but he was grinning like a cat with a brand new mouse when he climbed into the ring.

"Who wants to go first?" Butchie asked.

Teddy bounced forward while I was still trying to say "Me" and Butchie said okay and gloved him up. We wore 16 ounce gloves, big as pillows. Teddy and I had laced them up before to hit the heavy bag but this was the first time either of us was going to try them out on someone who hit back.

Antoine waited in the ring, bouncing in place in his corner. Teddy stepped through the ropes as Max arrived to referee the match. He tossed Butchie a brand new rubber mouthpiece to stuff into Teddy's mouth.

"That's to keep you from swallowing your teeth." Butchie said giving Teddy an encouraging pat on the shoulder. Teddy glanced over at me. His eyes looked a little wider than usual.

That done Max called them both to the center of the ring and said,

"Okay you guys, I want you to go easy. Remember what you've been taught, nobody gets hurt. Got it?"

They nodded, mouths full of rubber and returned to their corners. Gradually all other activity in the gym halted. Several fighters wandered over to ringside, others watched in place from where they were working out. Butchie clanged a ringside bell and Teddy marched out to face Antoine.

Antoine started slow, a couple of light jabs which drove Teddy's gloves back into his face. Teddy shook this off but still didn't throw a punch. Antoine rattled off a quick left, right, left combination to Teddy's head and body which rocked him back on his heels.

"Move around Teddy, let him know you're there." Butchie offered. My throat was so dry I couldn't say a word. Teddy took his eyes off Antoine for just a second to look over at Butchie and Antoine landed a roundhouse left to Teddy's head. Teddy staggered, dropped his hands and Antoine punished him with two quick jabs to the face. A slow trickle of blood started to run from Teddy's nose. Antoine backed mercifully away as Teddy pulled himself together.

Antoine started forward and as he got closer Teddy uncorked a roundhouse left hand that caught Antoine off guard. The punch landed with a solid smack and Antoine retreated. Teddy came forward, as he should have and ran right into two more jabs to the face and a solid right hand to the body. Teddy sagged, the bell rang and both fighters returned to their corners.

Butchie yanked the mouthpiece out of Teddy's mouth and asked, "You okay? You wanna' keep going?"

Teddy was huffing and puffing, his chest going in and out like an overworked balloon. His nose had stopped bleeding.

"Yeah, yeah, I'm okay." Teddy half gasped, sucking in as much air as he could. Butchie crossed the ring to where Antoine was seated in his corner. Max looked on carefully, holding Antoine's mouthpiece.

"You okay?" Butchie asked.

"Yeah, yeah, forgot he was a dukie, he's got a good punch." Antoine responded. Butchie stuffed Antoine's mouthpiece back in and then did the same for Teddy. He hit the bell for round two.

Teddy more than survived the next two rounds, tiring considerably by round three but Antoine backed off, dancing around him and offering only light jabs as reminders to keep his hands up. When round three ended Max called them both to the center of the ring.

"Nice fight, both of you. Antoine, you got three more?"

Antoine looked relaxed, he had hardly broken a sweat. Teddy was gassed, but happy. He and Antoine tapped gloves and Butchie looked at me and said, "Get ready."

I didn't do well, I didn't do badly. Antoine clearly could have ended me a half dozen, no, a whole dozen times, but he held off. I tried to remember all I had been told.

"Get tired punching, not defending."

"Watch your opponent's eyes, they'll tell you everything he's going to do."

"Take the fight to him, don't let him take it to you."

"Stay on your feet. Stay focused. Breathe."

"Chin down, elbows in, don't bleed."

At the end of my three rounds I was completely exhausted and moderately satisfied. Antoine had tagged me just enough to let me know getting hit wouldn't kill me. I had landed a jab or two, even a wayward right hand now and then and most importantly I was still standing at the fight's end.

As Butchie unlaced my gloves I noticed the guys in the gym were looking at Teddy and me differently. We had passed a test, no longer tourists, there was acceptance in their glances. We weren't jamokes.

"Conditioning," Butchie said as me and Teddy sat rubber legged and exhausted on a ringside bench. "A month ago you guys wouldn't have lasted two minutes in there. You did good. Keep training, I'm proud of you." Butchie left, Max walked over.

"You guys owe me a buck each for the mouthpieces, unless you want to borrow someone else's." We didn't. "Double up on the heavy bag this week. You win when you punch. Punch hard you win faster. You both did pretty good for your first time out. Next time Antoine's not gonna' dance with you so much, neither is anybody else. Good job."

Max walked off and Teddy and I sat basking in self-satisfaction. A few minutes later Antoine came over.

"Good fight you guys. You okay?"

Teddy and I said, "Yeah," and Antoine sat down next to us.

"You caught me by surprise with that left, you hit hard." That got a big smile from Teddy who thanked Antoine for the match, complimenting him on his speed and mobility. We chatted for a few minutes as I did the same and then Teddy excused himself to go to the latrine.

"So why'd you get kicked out of Keith?" Antoine asked when we were alone.

Funny thing, lots, and I mean lots of people had asked me if I was the guy who got kicked out of Keith, hardly anybody ever asked why.

"They didn't like me much there." I responded, short answer.

"Shee-it man, lots of people round here don't like you, don't mean we're gonna' kick your ass out."

Didn't like me here? Antoine saw the look on my face and started laughing. He had this great laugh and made a sound like "ksk, ksk, ksk" while bouncing his head up and own.

"Relax, man, I was jokin', don't nobody here know you enough to like you or not, least ways I don't."

It mattered to me that people liked me, at least if certain people liked me. Here at the gym I wanted people to like me, I wanted Antoine to like me.

"Up at Keith they told me I wasn't Keith Academy material."

"What the hell's that? Keith Academy material? You an atiest or somethin'?"

"No nothing like that. I guess they meant I wasn't good enough for them."

I could say this now without bitterness or sadness, they were not the kind of people who I cared whether they liked me or not.

"Yeah, I got that, colored man been hearin' that since he's born seems like."

"Really? From who?" Without realizing how dumb I must have sounded.

Antoine drew back, as if surprised, even a little offended by my question. He considered me for a moment and replied, "You know when I used to go to school, all those years right up till eight grade I didn't never get called on in class, not once, even when I raised my hand to answer."

"You said when you used to go to school. Aren't you going to school now?"

"What for? Didn't nobody care when I was there."

"You quit school?" This was hard for me to get my head around.

"Didn't quit, just stopped goin', like I said, nobody cared."

"What about your mother and father? Didn't they care?"

"Didn't tell 'em, for a while. Got me a job out at the golf course, started earnin' a little money, help out with the bills." About then Teddy rejoined us.

"Lemme' ask you two sumthin', you know who Cassius Clay is?"

"Won the Gold Medal in the Olympics in Rome. Light heavyweight. Turned pro when he got home, he's undefeated, like 18-0. They say he's gonna' fight Sonny Liston for the championship next year." Teddy to the rescue. He read Sports Illustrated like Margaret Mary read the Encyclopedia Britannica. I knew the Gold Medal part.

"Know any other colored athletes?" Antoine asked.

"Willie Mays, number 24, best centerfielder in baseball, Hank Aaron, "Hammerin' Hank", Bill Russell, Boston Celtics, Jim Brown, Cleveland Browns, Floyd Patterson, Joe Lewis…"

"Whoa, whoa, whoa," Antoine laughed, "Dukie here knows his Negroes."

Dukies were guys who were left handed. The nick name stuck, at the gym Teddy was now "Dukie" or "The Duke". I was still the guy who got kicked out of Keith.

"Let me ask you somethin' else," Antoine added, "You know any colored doctors, colored lawyers, airline pilots, maybe? You see any colored folk on the TV who ain't openin' doors or carrying white folk's luggage?" I was embarrassed by my silence.

"Says somethin' 'bout why I ain't in school." Antoine stood up to go. "See you guys around the gym."

Teddy and I both realized we had just caught a glimpse of something we had never considered before.

That night I went over to Margaret Mary's. She was on her front porch, reading, as usual. Sean was in his den with textbooks and a glass of whiskey. I took my place on a porch chair and asked, "Do you know any colored people?"

Margaret Mary considered me for a moment, then answered, "I did in Chicago, but no, I don't know any colored people here in Lowell. Why do you ask?"

"I met this guy down at the gym…" I began.

"A colored guy?" Margaret Mary interrupted, "And by the way colored people now prefer to be called black."

"Okay, I met this black colored guy down at the gym…"

"Just black, not black colored guy." Margaret Mary was in teacher mode.

"You want me to tell this story or not?"

Margaret Mary folder her hands in her lap and nodded. I continued,

"His name is Antoine Davis. I boxed three rounds with him today and he was nice enough not to knock me out."

Now Margaret Mary was leaning forward, inspecting me, I presume, for welts and bruises.

"Antoine asked me if I knew a black doctor or lawyer, teacher, anything like that and I was really embarrassed to say that I didn't. In fact, I think Antoine is the first black guy I ever talked to about stuff." This was sounding worse the more I thought about it.

"About stuff? Or at all?" Margaret Mary asked.

Again, I was embarrassed to say 'at all", but I wasn't sure why. "Does this mean I'm like prejudiced or something?" I felt kind of foolish asking but the thought that I might be, or actually was, had never occurred to me.

"First of all," Margaret Mary offered, "I don't believe you're prejudiced, you are too intelligent for that. It's just that Lowell does not have a large or very visible black community."

"I think there are some colored people living over on Hale Street." I offered.

This was more urban legend than fact, in actuality I could not name or find a place in my hometown where colored, or black people lived. I did know that they were seldom seen in the schools I attended. None, not one in eight years of grade school, none at Keith Academy, two out of our whole high school class. I had never seen a black teacher, doctor, nurse, policeman, priest, nun or shopkeeper. Or perhaps I had just never noticed. I now tried to decide which was worse.

"I'm going to get you a book," Margaret Mary declared, "I'll be right back."

Margaret Mary always had a book, or knew about a book, it was as if she had the whole library memorized. She disappeared into the house as I racked my brain to remember the last time I had seen, or more accurately, noticed a black man or woman in Lowell. A bus driver perhaps? Or a garbage man? Janitor? Cook or waiter? Hazy, probabilities were the best I could manage.

Margaret Mary came back to the porch carrying a book which she passed to me.

"You must be careful with this, its Sean's, one of his favorites. He said we would talk about it after you finish."

I was looking at "Invisible Man", by Ralph Ellison. I knew this was not "The Invisible Man" from the movies, and I had read the book by H.G. Wells from which the movie was made. It was really good. This was something different I presumed.

"Have you read it?" I asked.

"I read it then forgot all about it until now. It sounds like you are starting to notice what this book is about and I am glad you reminded me. Now I have a question for you, are you going to the dance at the Commodore next weekend?"

Next weekend at the Commodore Ballroom there was going to be a dance with Freddie Cannon appearing. Freddie was a local singer who had hits like "Palisades Park" and "Transistor Sister" as well as "Twisting All Night Long" which I definitely had no intention of doing.

"No," I replied, "I don't want to go." And besides I had nobody to go with.

"Well you should," Margaret Mary added, "Donna Delancey told me she'd go with you if you asked her."

Donna Delancey lived right near us. She was in a couple of my classes at Lowell High. She was blond and very cute. But…
"Donna is in my history class. She thought George Washington gave the Gettysburg Address."

Which got a magical, musical laugh from Margaret Mary. When she stopped giggling she suggested, "Well if you ask her, and you should, just don't talk about history."

Blond and cute did fill a lot of gaps.

"Are you going with Kevin?" I asked.

"Yes, and it would be nice if we double dated."

New book, new date (maybe) and new insight into things that had always been right in front of my face. It was always worth a trip to Margret Mary's house.

That Saturday morning at the gym Antoine called me and Teddy over to where he was talking with a group of fighters, mostly black, all more friendly since Teddy and I had gotten into the ring. There were smiles and nods as we approached. Antoine made the introductions. "This here is The Duke," indicating Teddy who swelled right up with the intro. "And this here is Dave, he's …"

"The guy who got kicked out of Keith." I finished the sentence for him.

There was a chorus of "Yeah's" and "I heard that" before the biggest fighter in the group a six foot plus heavyweight said, "I am The Prince, Eddie Prince, but you can call me Prince, in fact, make that you better call me Prince."

Which got a round of laughter from the group. "Paco Barnes," said a light skinned, mulatto guy who was wearing bag gloves. He bumped fists with me and Teddy and stepped back. "Taylor," the next man said, "Reggie Taylor, middleweight." The last man in the group grunted without giving his name or offering his hand. Not unfriendly, but not friendly either. He walked away, heading for the speed bags.

"That's Screwloose," Antoine offered, "you best take notice of why we call him that."

I already had. This was now, officially and without compare the largest number of black people I had ever spoken with, or been introduced to, and at some level been accepted by. Afterward when I talked to Teddy he said exactly the same thing.

"Hey Duke," Paco Barnes said, "How 'bout I talk to Max see if he let you and me go a few rounds later. I'm fighting a dukie down in Lawrence next week, you be helping me with my timing, circlin' round the proper way and such."

This was new stuff and not surprisingly Teddy was game. Max gave it the go ahead and later that afternoon I watched Teddy spar with Paco. They wore headgear and the big gloves. Teddy took some shots, not hard, Paco was working more on his footwork than his punch, but Teddy looked good in the ring, not a stranger out of place. He looked like a boxer. I hoped I could look the same way.

That week in school I asked Donna Delancey to the record hop. She said yes. In baseball language I was two for two, so far so good, at least until we found out what her father thought about guys who got kicked out of Keith. I was getting just a little paranoid about the subject.

At the gym Teddy and I had settled into a comfortable rhythm. Push-ups, sit ups, rope work, bags. Several times during our workouts Prince or one of the other guys would stop by and turn my shoulders a little on the big bag, or reposition Teddy's feet. Not a lot of words but enough to know they were watching and they cared about how we were doing. Butchie hung back a bit as we became more at ease with our new friends, our in the gym friends.

I caught up with Margaret Mary on Thursday at Brighams. I told her I was half through with Invisible Man and how uneasy I was with what I was reading. How had I never noticed any of this before? Why didn't I care? How come nobody told me? As usual Margaret Mary knew why.

"Nobody likes to talk about race in our country. It's a dirty little secret that is starting to change. You've seen the news stories about Martin Luther King, Ralph Abernathy, and the Freedom Riders in the South. Now they mean something, what they are doing matters, not just in the South, but here as well."

"I just never thought about it before," was the weakest and only excuse I could muster.

"There was never much for us to think about." She answered, "We're pretty sheltered here. That's good and that's bad."

Butchie, now Kevin, arrived just then and joined us at our table. He slid in next to Margaret Mary and slid his arm around her shoulders. I felt a pang but smiled.

"You tryin' to steal my girl?" He asked pleasantly.

"She was my girl first," popped out of my mouth in what I hoped sounded like a joke, which it wasn't.

"I am not anybody's girl," Margaret Mary declared laughing, "You are both very special to me, only in different ways." And I imagined she snuggled a little but closer to Butchie as another pang rattled me.

"You comin' to the dance Saturday with us?" Butchie, now Kevin, asked.

"Yeah, with Donna Delancey." Which got a smile from Margaret Mary.

"She's a cutie," Butchie offered, "Smart too I heard." Which got another smile from Margaret Mary.

"Kevin, can I ask you a question?" This had been on my mind.

"Sure," he slipped his arm out from around Margaret Mary and leaned forward on the table.

"Those guys at the gym, Antoine and the others, you ever hang out with them when you're not at the gym?"

Butchie, now Kevin, thought this over for a minute. "Well, not really, I mean sometime I see them around you know, but I can't say I hang out with them."

"Why not?" Margaret Mary and I asked at almost the same time.

Butchie, now Kevin leaned back in the booth, blew out a long breath and looked from Margaret Mary to me, perhaps deciding how to answer.

"You pay, what? Five bucks a month to work out at the gym?" I nodded.

"So do I. You get the money from your folks, right?"

Again I nodded though I was starting to get uncomfortable with my answers.

"Don't get me wrong," he said, "That's a good thing. I'm sure your parents are good people and give you money because they want you to be able to do things you want to do. I work ten hours a week at Northeast Paper Box, loading trucks, sweeping up, stacking pallets, factory stuff. I get a buck seventy five an hour. That's how I pay Max."

"I'm gonna' start working at Lefty's Drive In this summer, as soon as school gets out." I offered defensively.

"I'm not talkin' about how you, or me, or Maggie gets money. That's not the point."

More cynical people than I would state that how one gets money is always the point, but that was not what Butchie, now Kevin was aiming at.

"Antoine, down at the gym, he stays late after the gym is closed. Sweeps up, empties buckets, cleans, whatever. He doesn't have five bucks, not to spare anyway. He caddies out a Longmeadow summers and works maintenance around there the rest of the year. I don't know what he gets an hour, but it ain't much."

He paused, unsure of whether to go on. He sounded like he was getting mad. Margaret Mary put her hand on his arm. He continued, "Antoine's got six brothers and sisters. Two older brothers, an older sister and three younger than him. The clothes he's wearing now his older brothers wore last year and the year before. He stopped going to school after the eighth grade and one day I asked him why. Know what he said?"

I was all ears, really, I wanted to know, a lot. I knew Margaret Mary was fully tuned in as well.

He said, "Ain't no need for a lot of education if you're going to be a janitor."

It took me a long, sad minute to realize what he was saying was true.

Butchie, now Kevin looked around and continued, "We got what, two vanilla cokes here, fifteen cents each, dime for the coffee, dime for the tip, fifty cents, right? Antoine's got to eat lunch for that, two days. He gives most of his money to his mother to help out. His father works down at the train yard probably not making eighty bucks a week. But lack of money is not why I don't hang out with Antoine. Poor is about a lot more than how much money a guy has."

Margaret Mary and I were stone silent, our vanilla cokes untouched.

Butchie, now Kevin went on, "The Prince? Eddie, he busts tires at the truck stop out on Route 3. He gets nuthin' an hour, fifty cents a tire. You ever try to bust a truck tire off a rim? It ain't easy. Paco works full time over at Tony's in Centerville. They'd fire him if they found out he's only fifteen. I don't know what Screwloose does, I'm afraid to ask him."

"There is a person you two know named Screwloose?" Margaret Mary sounded worried.

"Down at the gym," I replied. "Teddy is now 'The Duke' by the way." Margaret Mary shook her head.

Butchie, now Kevin continued, "Count how many black kids you're gonna' see at the Commodore this Saturday. I'll do it for you, none. You ever see any black people in Brighams?"

Without waiting for us to answer he continued, "Why not? You think black people don't like ice cream?" This question a little sharper than the first. Margaret Mary put her hand on his arm again. He seemed to relax a bit.

"I'm sorry," he said, "I don't hang around with the guys at the gym because I think I'm better than them. I don't hang around black people because I don't like them. I don't hang around with them because I know they're strugglin' a lot harder to get by than me and they don't have the same opportunities and privileges that I do, and I know there's not a damn thing I can do about it, or even will do about it, it just is. They know the deal, we know the deal. They resent us

because of what we have, we feel uncomfortable because we have it
and they don't."

He grew silent, like a steam engine resting. The silence hovered at
our table until Margaret Mary asked, "Why is it different at the gym?
You guys all seem to get along there."

Which was a very good question, one I had only begun to think about.
Butchie, now Kevin took a breath and answered, "Max's gym is one
thing, separate. I mean everybody who wants to train gets a chance
there. Black or white. When Dave and Teddy walked in I gave them
a week, maybe. But they did the work. Boxing is hard, lots of guys
start but don't stay. Black or white if you stay you get treated the
same. Too bad all that stops when you walk out the door."

And from that afternoon on things changed for me. I noticed an
elderly black couple, arm in arm, coming out of the Bon Marche
department store. They were hunched over against the chill March
wind just like everybody else, but different. I saw a cab driver,
chewing on a toothpick, his face and arms shiny black through the taxi
window. When I went over to St. Joseph's hospital to visit my sick
cousin I saw the maid staff and janitors of the hospital, almost
exclusively black, going about their business as if they weren't really
there. I realized there was a deep, significant difference in the way I
was seeing now as opposed to the way I saw the streets and people of
Lowell before. The lack was not just in me, I now knew, but in the
system itself, ours and theirs. When I finished Mr. Griffin's stunning
book and learned more, much more than I ever thought to know about
the huge differences in the lives of black and white Americans, I put
the information aside, stored it for later, though I knew not when that
later would ever be. Despite those insights I was awash with everyday
matters, there was school work, a daily dose of responsibility to my
teachers, my parents and myself. Every night after homework the TV
beckoned. There were different favorites for each evening; a parade
of gunslingers, marshals, crusading lawyers and doctors and even
bubbly bandleaders a-one and a-two and a-threeing their way through
our evening's entertainment. I barely noticed they were all White
Like Me.

I continued to look forward to and enjoyed training at the gym. Teddy, now The Duke, and I had begun sparring regularly with other fighters and holding our own, keeping the beat and sharing the smiles and satisfaction that came with a job well done. Max himself had officially announced that we were not jamokes. And there was Donna Delancey. She may not have been the brightest girl but she loved to dance slow, real slow, and very close. One almost spring day when we were at her house alone she decided to show me her brand new two piece bathing suit. Not show me like on a hangar, she put it on. In the house where we were alone. What ensued was what best could be described as something I was not yet ready to talk about even with Margaret Mary.

As green grass started to poke its way through scattered clumps of leftover April snow my thoughts turned to baseball season and weekend trips to York Beach with my family. I had also started working the counter at Lefty's Drive In, taking orders and filling counter drinks. Gradually there was less time for the gym. I saw less of Antoine and The Prince, Paco and the others. Though I tried not to think about it I realized that the changing of the seasons meant much less to them. There were no weekend fishing trips, summer ball games under the lights with ice cream afterward. Though I had become more aware of the black men and women and families in Lowell, and I genuinely liked the guys at the gym, I was not connected to them in any way outside of the gym. The orbit of my life held much greener pastures and greener pastures were where I wanted to spend my time. Still a passage haunted me from Mr. Griffin's book. I had copied it by hand into my school notebook and read it every once in a while to remind me. The passage reads…

The Negro's only salvation from complete despair lies in his belief, the old belief of his forefathers, that these things are not directed at him personally, but against his race, his pigmentation. His mother or aunt or teacher long ago carefully prepared him, explaining that he, as an individual, can live with dignity, even though he, as a Negro, cannot. "They don't do it to you because you're Johnny – they don't even know you. They do it against your negro-ness."

I read this to remind myself that the privileges I enjoyed because of my whiteness are intended for all people, regardless of pigmentation.

I read this to remind myself that I had been dealt a pretty good hand compared to many others. I kept this near me to remind myself to pay more attention to things I did not see. I remembered my humiliation and anger at being told I was not "Keith Academy Material" and compared this to the everyday experience of the black men and women of my city. Were they not, "Lowell Mass Material?"
All of this I could not answer but in the meantime there was Gunsmoke, Palladin and Lawrence Welk. And Donna Delancey.

"The Negro needs the white man to free him from his fears. The white man needs the Negro to free him from his guilt."

Martin Luther King

Chapter 19

SUMMER ON FIRE

The summer of 1963 was the time when everything around me seemed to catch fire. When the school year ended and the warm summer days rolled in, events, personal and nationwide seemed to heat up, become more intense, more complicated, and more relevant.

Margaret Mary and Kevin broke up. He became very upset with her decision to leave Keith Hall after two years and the argument ended in their breakup. When we spoke about the matter she told me it was not his concern that bothered her it was his presumption that he had a right to tell her what to do and did not respect her reasons for leaving. It wasn't so much that Margaret Mary didn't like being told what to do, but she definitely didn't like the lack of respect for her decision. But I already knew that.

Teddy quit the Red Sox. He was hanging out more at the gym and had become buddies with Antoine and Paco and a few other guys. Buddies outside the gym, something I had never mastered. A funny thing happened when Teddy started spending more time with Antoine and the others, he began adopting their mannerisms, rhythms of speech, idiosyncrasies and habits. Some of this was good, some not so much. He started smoking, a bad habit for a boxer, and his brother, Chris, would have killed him if he found out. But Chris had disappeared that summer. He told Teddy he couldn't take fighting with the "Old Man" any more and had to leave before something bad happened. I know Teddy missed Chris a lot, though I felt he was not filling that void in the best possible way. Teddy, now The Duke, was still my buddy, always would be, but he had stepped back a bit and our paths were drifting apart.

I still got along with Antoine and The Prince, I even had a few conversations with Screwloose which I partially understood. However baseball season had begun and that is where my focus shifted. More time at the ball field meant less time at the gym and a gap in our friendship developed. I missed hanging out with Teddy, missed seeing him over my shoulder in the outfield and batting just ahead of me in the lineup.

Peter Rayburn returned to Lowell for the summer. After being kicked out of Keith (with me) his parents sent him to Phillips Academy in Andover.

Phillips was a big deal, an exclusive, kind of famous school. Humphrey Bogart had gone there and gotten kicked out, which I of course thought was cool. So did Edgar Rice Burroughs who wrote all the Tarzan books. There was a long line of distinguished alumni from Phillips and Peter had flourished since transferring there. Apparently "Why" was not a dirty word in their classrooms.

He returned a firebrand, burning with an awareness and devotion to current social issues. He spoke fluently of the powerful concerns of the day, civil rights, the ongoing hostility with the Soviet Union and of the smoldering and dangerous unrest in a small Asian country I had barely heard of, South Vietnam.

One Saturday morning while I was working at Lefty's, Peter came in. He had taken to wearing a lot of black and, I swear to God, a beret. He had a serious, semi-angry air about him that did not serve him well. But we were still buddies from Shedd Park and I was glad to see him. He was sitting at a back table nursing a cup of coffee and a paperback book when I took my break and came to sit with him.

"You're a working man now?" He offered.

"Tuesdays, Thursdays and Saturdays," I answered pulling up a chair. "What'cha reading?"

Peter waved the paperback at me, "Steppenwolf, it's about the duality of human nature, might be a little too heavy for you."

Wow, condescending and insulting, Peter hadn't lost his touch.

"So how do you like Phillips? Is it a good school?" I asked, changing the subject.

"Good school, great school. They really seem to care about what they teach."

"You playing any ball down there?"

Peter looked at me like he smelled something bad. "Really Dave, with all that is going on in the world do you think I have any time for playing ball?" With all that was going on in the world I thought it was essential to make time to play ball, but this was not an argument I wanted to start with Peter. "Besides," he continued, "I don't have time for a lot of kid stuff."

"Sorry to hear you say that Pete. You played a really good second base."

Which seemed to loosen him up a bit. He put down the book and the attitude.

"Yeah, I miss it sometime. You still playing?"

"All I can, but you're right, it's hard to find the time now."

"How's Teddy?" He asked. "I haven't seen him around much."

"Teddy is now 'The Duke'," I answered with a smile, "He hangs out down at Nelson's Gym a lot. He's a pretty good boxer."

"Boxer? I didn't see that in Teddy, you maybe, but not Teddy."

"I went with him for a while," I admitted, "Liked it too, but with school and all I had to let it go."

"Well Teddy would never have that problem, school and all." Peter was back to condescending and insulting.

"Teddy's not stupid," I reacted, getting a little tired of Peter's attitude.

"Yeah, you're right," Peter said almost apologetically. "I didn't mean it that way, it's just that Teddy was never one to prioritize school, not like we did anyway. Do you still see Margaret Mary?"

"Always," I answered, a little too quickly. Peter didn't seem to notice.

"I heard she dropped out of Keith Hall."

"Resigned, wrote them a letter, told them she was disappointed in the school and chose not to continue." I answered with pride in my voice.

"That's the way we should have gone." Peter said, sadly.

"Yeah," I answered. "You still think about it?"

"You bet," the anger returning to his tone, "They had no right to treat me, or you, that way."

"Well, I guess they had the right," I offered, "but it still pisses me off too."

"It was enough I had to put up with the religious nonsense and the snobbery but the hypocrisy of those bastards," Peter was heating up, "Taught me a valuable lesson." He sighed, taking a breath.

"What lesson was that?" I wasn't sure I had learned one.

"It taught me to examine carefully what the rules are before I decide to obey them and it taught me that when something really bad happens, like kicking us out, that maybe something good will happen because of it. You know what I mean?"

"Like what?" I asked.

"Well, I really like where I'm going to school now. I'm learning a lot more than I would have at Keith and I'm learning to say what's on my mind without worrying so much what other people think about it."

Those were good things, no doubt about it but there was more acid in Peter's tone now, not a good thing. The duality of human nature.

"How long you home for?" I asked.

"Two more weeks then I'm going back for summer session so I can graduate early."

"Why do you want to graduate early?"

"College, Dave, college is where your real education begins. High school is mostly memorization and agreeing with your teachers. College is when you get to do the real stuff."

The real stuff, whatever that was, was something I had not given a lot of thought to. Even Margaret Mary, my North Star for such questions had been too awash in Keith Hall issues and Butchie, now Kevin, questions to look that far down the road. Peter apparently had, and I realized this was a subject that needed tending to, but my break was over and I had to get back to work. Standing away from the table I had to ask,

"Pete, what's with the beanie?"

Peter grinned his wolf grin and said, "I like it a lot, it really seems to annoy people."

Same old Peter.

So I worked the counter at Lefty's that summer making milk shakes and frappes, pouring cokes and coffee and taking orders for food. Work and Babe Ruth League Baseball filled my days and nights while graphic and horrific images exploded from the TV of police dogs being loosed on black marchers in Selma, Alabama, coupled with scenes of Buddhist Monks setting themselves afire in the streets of a faraway city named Saigon.

Later that summer Governor, George Wallace, took a stand blocking the schoolhouse door at the University of Alabama vowing, "segregation now, segregation tomorrow, segregation forever". To end this bigotry President Kennedy sent US Attorney General Nicholas Katzenbach and a Brigadier General from the Alabama National Guard to order him to "stand down" and allow the enrollment of black students at the university. When he stood aside the first ever black students were admitted to the University amidst screams of hatred and prejudice.

Rock & Roll, my inner heartbeat was changing as well. Margaret Mary had bought an album, "The Freewheelin' Bob Dylan" and insisted that I listen, attentively, to "Blowing In The Wind" and "A Hard Rain's A-Gonna Fall" warbled in a voice that sounded like a cat being dragged through a keyhole. But it was not the voice Margaret Mary was calling my attention to, it was the words like...

How much do I know
To talk out of turn
You may say that I'm young

You may say I'm unlearned
But there's one thing I know
Though I'm younger than you
That even Jesus would never
Forgive what you do.

These from "Masters of War" another track on this album. I listened and realized this was different than anything I had heard before. Different good or different bad was something I had not decided yet.

One thing I did know, or thought I did, was that this guy, Bob Dylan, was not going to get way with singing things like that for very long. Not while the Four Seasons were telling us to "Walk Like A Man" and Edie Gorme was explaining that we could "Blame It On The Bossa Nova". Still, more melodious performers like Peter, Paul and Mary were starting to sing "Blowing In The Wind" and "Puff The Magic Dragon" while the Kingston Trio asked "Where Have All The Flowers Gone?" Whatever was going on was a far cry from "Be-Bop-A-Lu-La" and "You Ain't Nuthin' But A Hound Dog", though Nat King Cole assured us we could still enjoy those, "Lazy, Hazy, Crazy Days of Summer". Not so much.

I too had my summer break up, with Donna Delancey. By me this time. Donna was way too willing to approach the joys of motherhood, which would have made me parent number two, and when I finally worked up the courage to discuss this with Margaret Mary she was shocked, really shocked, at the intensity of my physical relationship with Donna. We had bypassed "making out" at a hundred miles an hour and I was smart enough to be wary, terrified actually of what could happen next.

When Margaret Mary's eyes had returned to about half their normal size, and she caught her breath, we talked about responsibilities and our plans for the future that did not include parenthood before I had my driver's license. She was, as always, the voice of reason, and caution, and common sense that I had put aside in a rush of hormones. Sex, the great oncoming mystery, was best left, we decided, for future years and wiser times. I so much needed to hear this. I knew I was on very dangerous ground with Donna but without Margaret Mary to counsel me I could have drifted into very deep water. And drowned.

So one night as I was half listening to Donna's monologue about her favorite color unicorn, I broke up with her. There were tears, hers, and my, "It's not you, it's me" explanation which I would repeat many times in the future, and the deed was done. I had looked paternity in the eye and gotten away safely. I hoped.

I ran into Butchie, now Kevin, one afternoon down city and he filled me in on all the latest goings on at the gym, Teddy's progress as a boxer and the like. Then he asked, "How's Margaret Mary doing?"

Fine, I wanted to say but within me there was a fear I might rekindle his interest in her, my girl I never told anyone about.

"She's you know, busy." I answered. "She's helping Sean put together a book of Irish poetry."

"Yeah," Butchie, now Kevin, laughed, "That was the thing about Margaret Mary and me. She was always reading some book I had never heard of, or talking about some artist I didn't know. She's a great girl but I always felt kind of, well, dumb, I guess, around her."

"Me too", I agreed. "But that's not always a bad thing, you know?"

"It is if you have to stack pallets on a loading dock every Saturday and hit the bag four days a week. I couldn't keep up, but I have to admit I never felt like she thought she was better than me or anything. Like I said, she's a great girl."

Yeah, I thought, I know.

"How come you two never got together? You think it's a big secret people can't tell you're nuts about her?"

It shows? People can tell? I didn't know what to say. Butchie, now Kevin, laughed.

"Hey, relax, I was just curious, you know?"

"We're like, friends, you know?" I stammered turning for some reason red as a traffic light.

"Well you ought'a be more than that. She's a great girl."

Butchie, now Kevin, sauntered off leaving me smack dab in the middle of my confusion about Margaret Mary.

One balmy summer evening about a week after I ran into Butchie now Kevin, Margaret Mary and Sean rang the front doorbell of my home. We were surprised to see them, a weeknight visit, slightly out of the ordinary. Sean was carrying a sheaf of papers and said he had something he would like to share with us.

Sean was in earnest, stone cold sober, holding Margaret Mary's hand on our front porch. When my Mom ushered them in we gathered in the living room. My Dad shut off the TV. My two brothers retreated to the back bedroom to pout. Sean explained, "Only a short time ago we gathered here in your home and watched what could have very easily become the end of the world."

I knew he was speaking of what was now being called "The Cuban Missile Crisis" and I remembered the looks of fear on my parents faces as we "camped out" in our basement for two days while tensions escalated, warships gathered and bombers, loaded with nuclear weapons, circled in the sky.

"I was grateful then that you opened your home to us," Sean put his arm around Margaret Mary, "during that distressing time. Our President himself, John Fitzgerald Kennedy, made a speech today at the American University in Washington, D.C. It was a beautiful speech but not one you would likely hear on your TV. I have a transcript of his words which was sent to the college today. I would like to share it with you this evening if you will permit me."

Sean had our attention now and our permission, as he continued, "This is, in part, what our President had to say this afternoon to the graduates of our National University,

"I have, therefore, chosen this time and place to discuss a topic on which ignorance too often abounds and the truth is too rarely perceived - yet it is the most important topic on earth – World Peace.

What kind of peace do I mean? What kind of peace do we seek? Not a Pax America enforced on the world by American weapons of war. Not a peace of the grave of the security of the slave. I am talking about genuine peace, the kind of peace that makes life on earth worth living, the kind that enables men and nations to grow and to hope and to build a better life for their children – not merely peace for Americans but peace for all men and women – not merely peace in our time but peace for all time."

Sean went on to read, in reverent tones the complete text of our President's words. They were words of promise and hope and understanding that laid the groundwork for a Nuclear Test Ban Treaty, a partnership with Russia to end the threat of cataclysmic nuclear war. It was a good speech, a great speech and which concluded with these words...

"The United States, as the world knows, will never start a war. We do not want a war. We do not now expect a war. This generation of Americans has already had enough – more than enough – of war and hate and oppression. We shall be prepared if others wish it. We shall be alert to try and stop it. But we shall also do our part to build a world of peace where the weak are safe and the strong are just. We are not helpless before that task or hopeless of its success. Confident and unafraid we labor on – not toward a strategy of annihilation but toward a strategy of peace."

When he finished reading Sean held Margaret Mary close and added, "Since it was here, in this very room, we gathered to hear of nuclear destruction at our doorstep I wanted to bring this message here that we may know that perhaps higher angels and better hearts have prevailed and the doom is now behind us."

We sat in grateful agreement. My Mom served tea. My brothers ventured out of the back room and a soft summer evening blew pleasantly past our front door.

It was a summer of speeches, great speeches from our leaders about important subjects, cherished ideals, lofty goals, and what's more they now seemed to apply to us, to me, demanding not just admiration and respect but somehow my participation in the ambitions they outlined.

President Kennedy and his wife seemed to be everywhere that summer. Sailing on Cape Cod, attending church services at the National Cathedral, hosting elegant state dinners at the White House, the President and First Lady presided over what had come to be called Camelot in Washington, D.C. With glamor and grace they offered hope amidst the increasing chaos of world affairs and we followed their every movement.

As that summer wore on President Kennedy delivered yet another message of hope as he outlined the Civil Rights legislation he proposed to bring equality in a nation founded on the principle, but not, as yet, the practice, of all men being created equal. In a nationally televised address on radio and television President Kennedy said...

"We preach freedom around the world, and we mean it, but are we to say to the world, and, much more importantly to each other, that this is the land of the free except for the Negroes?"

"This is not a sectional issue. Difficulties over segregation and discrimination exist in every city, in every state of the union, producing in many cities a rising tide of discontent that threatens the public safety."

The very next day, Medgar Evers, the field secretary of the Mississippi NAACP was murdered by members of the Ku Klux Klan. The summer on fire burned ever brighter.

Teddy came by one of my Babe Ruth games one night accompanied by Antoine and The Prince. I hadn't seen any of those guys in quite a while and I was glad to see them. When I doubled deep to left in the fourth inning Teddy was on his feet clapping when I slid into second. Two runs scored and Antoine and The Prince were clapping as well. Baseball, as always, felt terrific.

After the game we caught up with each other.

"You looking good out there." The Prince offered.

"Thanks, how are you guys? Still punchin?"

"Punchin' hard my brother," Antoine added, "These are harsh times."

Harsh times they were but somehow on the sideline at O'Donnell Field didn't seem like the place to get into that.

"You hear anything from Chris?" I asked Teddy.

"Nah," he answered, "Wish I did."

"When you comin' back to the gym?" Antoine asked.

"This fall, after baseball. I'll have more time. I miss you guys."

"Don't miss us enough," The Prince said, "Don't see you around."

"I haven't been around. I'm a working man now."

"Working man, playing ball, you been around," Antoine noted, "Just not around us."

We shared a laugh but I knew what Antoine was talking about. Greener pastures.

I had to go, my Mom and Dad and brothers were waiting for me by the car. We were off to Nichol's Ice Cream for a post-game cone. Teddy, Antoine and The Prince wandered off toward Hale Street. As they left I remembered what Butchie, now Kevin had said a long time ago in Brighams.

"You think black people don't like ice cream?"

Later that summer President Kennedy travelled to Berlin, the city in Germany torn in half by a Soviet wall of barbed wire and concrete which divided the city into Communist dominated and Free World zones. In a speech given in the shadow of this wall President Kennedy declared, "Ich bin ein Berliner", pledging our support and unity with the besieged people of West Berlin. Our President continued to show himself not merely as our national leader but as a world leader. His fire never went out.

In August, Dr. Martin Luther King, speaking at the Lincoln Memorial in Washington, D.C. made his "I Have A Dream" speech before an estimated crowd of over 250,000 people.

Great events swirled about, great words were being spoken, great leaders were emerging as summer faded and the oaks and elms began to show their autumn colors. Yet one event above all others and unnoticed by all but me and mine took place one evening when I sat with Margaret Mary on her front porch. We spoke of minor things, who was dating who, my job at Lefties, the poetry of the Irish and Sean's devotion to his new book.

Summer was fading and Labor Day weekend approached. I asked Margaret Mary if she was nervous about coming to Lowell High in a few weeks.

"A little," she admitted, "but you will be there and that will make it alright."

"You should try and get Mr. Parker for English Lit. He's funny and he knows lots of good books."

"Mr. Parker," she made a mental note, "anybody else?"

"We should try and get classes together. I always do better when you are in the room." I added.

"That would be nice. Is there anyone else you are trying to get in classes with?"

"You mean like teachers?" I asked.

"No, like girls. Barbara or Donna maybe?"

"Barbara's going out with Paul Sanders now. Donna came into Lefty's a few weeks ago, wouldn't even look at me."

"That is definitely for the better," Margaret Mary answered.

An end of summer dance was being held at the Commodore Ballroom. I had no date and Margaret Mary had not reconciled with Butchie, now Kevin, so I asked her if she was going to go.

"No", she replied. "I don't want to go alone or with the other girls so I think I will sit this one out."

"Maybe," I offered, "If you want, we could go together, but you could like, dance with anybody you wanted to when we were there."

"Aren't you going with Teddy?"

"Teddy's not going, he says he's doin' all his dancing in the ring now."

Margaret Mary considered me for a moment and replied, "Well, we will go together, but I will dance only with you."

And my heart, as the saying goes, skipped a beat.

Chapter 20

THE END

Dallas, Texas, November 22, 1963

The football flavored fall of 1963 strolled into Lowell with untold thousands of leaves of gold, brown, orange and burgundy painting our trees and blanketing our lawns. The air became cool and crisp, the sky deep blue, our sweaters and jackets warm and comfortable as the summer receded gracefully into winter.

The school year had begun. Margaret Mary and I shared three classes including Mr. Parker's English Literature course. On her first day at Lowell High Margaret Mary had paused before entering the crowded hallway leading to her home room.

Without a word she took my hand, just as she had so many years ago in the Strand theatre. Take that once again, Mr. Crockett.

A group of teenagers out of Hawthorne, California gave us "Surfin' USA", "Little Deuce Coupe" and "Surfer Girl" while Bobby Vinton crooned "Blue Velvet" and Martha and the Vandellas sang about a "Heat Wave." Rock and Roll was alive and well, sort of, while that Bob Dylan guy sharpened his chops and made ready to take American music in a whole new direction.

Teddy fought in his first Boxing Tournament, winning a split decision over a feisty fighter from Tewksbury named "Kid Gallavan". The Duke could punch.

On TV, Richard Kimble began his run as "The Fugitive" while Jed Clampett and clan were back for another year as "The Beverly Hillbillies". James Bond returned in "From Russia With Love" and the most expensive motion picture ever made, "Cleopatra", entertained and scandalized the movie public.

That summer President Kennedy made a movie star visit to Ireland appearing before adoring crowds wherever he went. He finished his triumphant four day visit with the message,

"I'm going to come back and see old Shannon's face again."

The Los Angeles Dodgers, behind their superstar lefty pitcher, Sandy Koufax, swept the New York Yankees 4-0 in the World Series and the Boston Celtics won their sixth straight NBA championship.

Peter Rayburn was elected junior year class president at Phillips Academy and was leading the school's debate team to a state championship, wearing his beret.

There was a Harvest Dance in October and Margaret Mary and I attended together, a couple. Teddy came as well, with a girl named Carol Saucier. They danced really well together. Butchie, now Kevin, came with Donna Delancey. She glowed, he looked exhausted. We sat at separate tables.

That same month, the nation celebrated the 1000th day of John Kennedy's Presidency. His approval ratings remained sky high and after his visit to Rome that summer for an audience with Pope Paul VI, criticism of JFK in our little corner of the world would unofficially be upgraded from a Venial Sin to a Mortal Sin. Supposedly.

In the South, Civil Rights issues intensified. The 16th Street Baptist Church in Birmingham, Alabama was bombed, during a religious service, leaving four dead and twenty-two injured. A month later singer Sam Cooke and his band were arrested in Louisiana for attempting to register in a "Whites Only" motel. And a black preacher named Malcom Little changed his name to Malcom X and began preaching about a "black revolution" to right these wrongs.

In faraway Saigon, on November 2, the President of South Vietnam, Ngo Dinh Diem, was assassinated and replaced by a military junta more inclined to aggressively wage the war against Communism. On November 11th, Veterans Day across America, President Kennedy places a wreath of flowers before the Tomb of the Unknown Soldier in Arlington National Cemetery. He later comments to Senator Hale Boggs of Louisiana,

"This is one of the really beautiful places on the earth. I could stay here forever."

Reports of wars and bombings, racial strife and communist aggression all diminished however as we anticipated the arrival of our upcoming Thanksgiving Holiday. Falling very late, on the 28th of November, the long weekend it promised would bring turkey, lots of turkey, family gatherings, pies, lots of pies, and football, lots of football.

Lowell High would play Lawrence High on Thanksgiving Day, the biggest and final game of the year for both schools. Margaret Mary and I would attend, along with practically the whole student body from both schools. No Turkey Dinner in our home was ever eaten until the final score had been posted, the winner congratulated and the sold out, jam packed stadium emptied for its winter slumber.

The long weekend which followed the Turkey Feast traditionally kicked off Christmas season and I began mentally compiling a list of gifts for my friends and family. Christmas lights and decorations would start going up all over town transforming Kearney Square to a twinkling wonderland. Christmas carols would be in the air.

All was right with the world as we sat in our afternoon classrooms, on the last Friday before Thanksgiving, November 22, 1963.

I was in Study Hall, not studying, when the long awaited school bell rang. I gathered my books, retrieved my jacket from my locker and found Margaret Mary for the walk home. We repaired from the school to the street corner across from the Big Clock and waited for Teddy to join us.

And then the sky fell in.

Along with the sun and the moon and the stars. Blue skies turned to gray, autumn to bleakest winter, serene anticipation to sudden shock all in the crack of an unheard gunshot.

"Somebody shot President Kennedy!"

Teddy shouted the news, scurrying across French Street where Margaret Mary and I waited for him.

Teddy was out of out of breath and frantic. All conversation stopped. All eyes turned to Teddy.

"I heard it on the radio in Mr. McHugh's office! All the teachers are in there! The radio said he was in Texas and somebody shot him!" The words tumbled out of Teddy, half shouted, half whispered.

Surely this could not be true. It was 2:08 PM, and all around us students swept by laughing and chatting, heading home for the weekend. Nobody seemed concerned, nobody seemed upset.

"Are you sure Teddy? Are you sure?" Margaret Mary asked. Nearby, several students stopped to listen. I was dumbfounded.

"I heard it I tell ya!" Teddy answered and suddenly there was a buzz on the street, groups of people clustered, some pointing at the school, searching about for verification of a rapidly spreading rumor.

"Come on," Margaret Mary pleaded, "We'll go to Spike and Tina's and see."

Spike and Tina's was a corner market directly across the street from The Immaculate Conception School and on our way home. We had

known them since our grade school years and behind their soda
fountain was a constantly flickering portable TV. Tina loved her
afternoon soap operas.

Hurrying up Merrimac Street everything appeared normal. Cars drove
past, people walked dogs and children, customers entered and exited
storefronts, but there was a hush, and a terrible foreboding being born
within us. When we got to Spike and Tina's store Tina was crying
hysterically behind the soda fountain. Three or four customers were
standing spellbound, staring at the small TV.

It was 2:19 PM. A reporter was standing in front of a hospital with a
microphone in his hand. He solemnly announced that President John
Fitzgerald Kennedy had been pronounced dead at 2PM Eastern
Standard Time, the exact time our school bell had rung releasing us
for the weekend.

On the TV scenes of wailing bystanders around Parkland Memorial
Hospital, where President Kennedy had been taken played against a
shaky and emotional announcement from CBS news man Walter
Cronkite…

*"The priest… who were with Kennedy… the two priests who were
with Kennedy, say that he is dead of his bullet wounds. That seems to
be as close to official as we can get at this time…"*

Margaret Mary eyes filled with tears, she buried her head in my
shoulder, shaking. A wail of grief yelped from Tina who turned from
the TV into the arms of her husband. It felt like all the air had been
sucked from the room. I looked at Teddy with dumb wonder as the
whole world seemed to go silent. There was a roaring in my ears that
could not shut out the words of Walter Cronkite who had suddenly
reappeared on the TV screen. Visibly shaken the veteran newscaster
repeated…

*"From Dallas Texas, a flash, apparently official, President Kennedy
died at 1PM Central Standard Time, 2PM Eastern Standard Time
some thirty-eight minutes ago."*

As we slowly refocused on the TV, Cronkite, his eyes full of tears and his voice shaking, went on…

"Vice President Lyndon Johnson has left the hospital in Dallas but we do not know where he has proceeded and presumably will be taking the oath of office shortly and will become the 36th President of the United States."

Nobody moved, nobody spoke. The TV droned on, the sound drowned out by the silence, yet continuing to offer images of grief stricken people crying in each other's arms, milling police cars, ambulances, confusion and chaos in Dallas.

"Why? Why would anybody do that?" Margaret Mary finally found her voice, pitched high and frantic with shock and sorrow. I held her still in my arms but could think of nothing to say.

For the next two hours we sat entranced at the soda fountain. The small portable TV updated our grief with images and hushed words as Air Force One waited to receive his body.

Ghastly images of Jacqueline Kennedy appeared and disappeared on the screen, her sorrow radiating from the oncoming darkness. Whispering newscasters chronicled the transportation of the President's body from Parkland Hospital to the Dallas airfield for the flight back to Washington.

We heard that aboard the plane Lyndon Johnson had been sworn in as the new president. We were informed that President Kennedy's body would be taken to Andrews Air Force Base outside of Washington, D.C. We watched the plane disappear into the Texas sky and we sighed, empty of all emotion save sadness and confusion.

"I betch'a the Russians did it," Teddy exclaimed, "or that Castro Guy."

By now rumors had started to circulate regarding the arrest of a man named Lee Harvey Oswald, an employee of the school book depository where the shots that killed our President apparently came from. He had been arrested for shooting a Dallas police officer named

J.D. Tippit outside a movie theatre less than an hour after President Kennedy's death. A rifle had been found on the sixth floor of the Texas School Book Depository where Oswald worked. The rest, for now, was all confusion.

As the afternoon crawled past full darkness fell. We had been at Spike and Tina's for almost three hours, unaware of the passing of time. Tina offered me her phone and I called home to tell my parents where we were. My Dad answered and said to stay right there, he would be right down to pick us up. We thanked Spike and Tina and waited outside for my Dad. Margaret Mary held my hand. None of us could think of anything to say. In a few minutes my Dad pulled up. Sean was with him. Sean looked like he had been crying.

We piled into the station wagon, solemn yet anxious to be leaving the place where we had witnessed such horrible events.

"Teddy, you're sister Connie called looking for you. I told her you'd be right home." My Dad said. Teddy thanked my Dad as I watched Margaret Mary keeping an eye on her father. He was strangely, ominously silent in the front seat staring out the side window.

"Sean are you alright?" She asked.

"No my darling daughter," he replied, in a choked whisper, "I am very far from alright in this most wretched circumstance."

Margaret Mary leaned forward and put her hand on her father's shoulder. He reached over and patted her hand but said nothing more. The rest of the ride home was silent but on the way my Dad pulled into Lefty's.

"I ordered fish dinners for supper," my Dad said. "Your Mom is too upset to cook. Teddy you're welcome to eat with us if you want." Lefty's Friday Night Fish Dinners were the best in the city, always a treat in our Catholic, no meat on Friday World. Tonight they would taste like clay, lumpen masses to be picked at and forgotten.

When we pulled into our driveway Teddy's father's battered blue truck was in their driveway. Teddy's father, Nick, was leaning against the hood, staring up at the sky. He didn't move or acknowledge us as we pulled in. Teddy, fearing perhaps that his father was angry with him, followed us into our house. Here another mournful newscast greeted us as we arrived. The volume turned low, my Mother and brothers sitting together on the living room sofa watching as ghostly images of Jackie Kennedy came and went as she was led from Air Force One to the waiting ambulance where her husband's body was being placed. Newscasters commented on her now blood spattered pink suit, all gray on our TV and our all gray world.

Sean moved silently to a chair in front of the TV, Margaret Mary went to sit with my Mother, Teddy followed my Dad and I into the kitchen. We placed the pink boxes of fish dinners in the oven and came to stand in the living room where now President Lyndon Johnson was about to make a speech to newsman at Andrews Air Force Base. The new president said,

"This is a sad time for all people. We have suffered a loss that cannot be weighed. For me, it is a deep personal tragedy. I know the world shares the sorrow that Mrs. Kennedy and her family bear. I will do my best, that is all I can do. I ask for your help, and God's."

And then Teddy said something I have never forgotten. He said, under his breath, "That guy looks like a crook to me."

There was a gentle knock at our front door. When my Mother answered she found Nick Gianoulous standing there. He too looked like he had been crying.

"Excuse me please," he said, "May I speak to my son, Theodoros?"

Teddy cautiously came from the kitchen to the front door. Nick Gianoulous' trademark anger had been smothered in sadness. No one said anything for a moment, then Nick said softly,

"Theo, your sister and I are going to the church to light a candle. Would you like to come?"

Without a word Teddy joined his father. As they turned to leave Nick turned to my Mother and said, "What kind of world is this we have brought our children into?" And they disappeared into the night.

Our dinners picked at and forgotten we watched President Kennedy's casket being carried into the White House. As political speculation began my Mother said, "Can we please turn that thing off? I've had all I can stand for one day."

So we did. I wanted to walk Margaret Mary home but she had taken Sean's arm when he rose from the chair and guided him to the front door. Though it was obvious he had been drinking he walked steadily to the front door where he turned to my parents and said,

"Thank you all very much for sharing your home and this time with us. I am overcome and fear this madness is only beginning."

I hugged Margaret Mary at our front door and they too disappeared into the night.

I went to bed that night envisioning the world once more on fire, only this time the flames burned low, simmering our sadness.

SATURDAY, NOVEMBER 23, 1963

The morning arrived with dreary reluctance. When I awoke I felt as tired as when I lay down the night before. I didn't want to leave my bed to confirm the sorrow that seemed to be waiting just outside my bedroom door, but breakfast sounds beckoned and I joined my Mother in the kitchen. The TV was not turned on. Gradually my Dad and my brothers appeared and we ate a silent breakfast. As we did the lure of the newscasts drew us to the living room.

Plates aside we turned on the TV and learned that the President's body was going to be ensconced at the White House for the remainder of the day for private family viewing. We were told that Jackie Kennedy had not left her the side of her husband's body until it was placed in the East Room of the White House and draped in black crepe. She then retired to her private quarters to rest. Speculation on a state funeral was discussed by still whispering newsman. We learned that while we slept Lee Harvey Oswald had been formally charged with President Kennedy's murder along with that of a Dallas Police Officer, J.D. Tippitt. No further details were available. The minutes dragged by.

Suddenly from within the fog that surrounded me I recalled it was Saturday, I was supposed to be at work at Lefty's in an hour.

"Dad, I'm supposed to work today. Do you think Lefty's is gonna be open?"

"I'm sure it will, son. People have to eat." He answered.

"I don't feel like going today, Dad." I was sad, too exhausted and sad to think about serving cokes and making frappes.

"Those people are counting on you. Get dressed, you should go to work as you promised."

So I did, but on the way I stopped by Margaret Mary's house. When I knocked on her front door nobody answered. The house was silent, perhaps they were still sleeping, as I wished I was. I tiptoed away not wanting to disturb their solitude.

In the house Margaret Mary watched in silence as I walked away. Later, much later, she would tell me that she could not face me, not anybody, on this gray, lifeless morning. She had watched her father drink himself unconscious after they left my house and cried to think of his deep sorrow. She watched the stars become hidden by clouds all night and when the morning came she could not feel the daylight. Alone in her home with her stricken father, she would spend the day in the company of Emily Dickinson who had written,

"After great pain, a formal feeling comes. The nerves sit ceremonious, like Tombs."

And that's how she told me she felt as I walked away from her house that morning.

At Lefty's business was grim but usual. People came in, ordered food, but there was no joy, no Saturday sparkle about the day. Lefty's had no TV, but local radio station WLLH played somber music with news updates of the planned public viewing of President Kennedy's body in Washington the next day. Tens of thousands, they said, were already lining up around the Capitol Building. There were hushed descriptions of tearful masses, openly crying women and silently sobbing men cueing up in a line that would eventually stretch for forty city blocks, waiting to enter the Rotunda where John Kennedy's body would lay in state. And the dirge continued.

Teddy came in to get lunch for him and his Dad at the Garage. Teddy said hardly anybody was coming in for gas and that there were very few cars on the street. He carried off his sandwiches and the day dragged on. There was none of our usual workplace banter, cheerful greetings from regular customers was nil, people just seemed to be going through the motions one eye or one ear on the goings on in Washington. The very sad goings on in Washington.

Later in the afternoon Peter Rayburn came in. No beret, no air of defiance, no vitality. He ordered coffee and repaired to a corner table. When I got the opportunity I joined him.

"Whadd'ya think of all this Pete? Pretty bad, huh?"

Peter looked at me like "pretty bad" was an idiot's way of describing what was going on. Peter could do that.

"When the president of the most powerful nation in the free world is murdered, in broad daylight, in an open car, sitting next to his wife, it is very much more than "pretty bad" don't you think?" Anger radiated off Peter like a highway flare, anger was his present go to emotion.

"Take it easy Peter, I'm as upset as you are, just not as pissed off." Sometimes Peter's attitude was hard to take, this was one of those times.

Peter blew out a breath and relaxed a bit. His shoulders sagged and he spoke in a lower voice, "Do you really think this guy Oswald shot

President Kennedy on his own? I doubt it very much. I believe there is something really evil going on here."

I hadn't really thought about any of that. I thought only of the loss, not what the loss meant. Peter's natural "Why?" attitude, coupled with his anger, was the way he was dealing with our immediate circumstances. I doubted that this was an improvement over the way I felt.

"How's Margaret Mary taking this? She was a pretty big fan of President Kennedy." Peter asked.

"Not good, she's very upset, so is her Dad. So is everybody else I know."

"Upset is just the beginning, mark my words." Peter finished his coffee and left, his words hanging in the already gloomy air. The beginning of what, I wondered, hoping I would never know.

Lefty closed the restaurant early, at 7 O'clock instead of the normal 11 PM. He said he was tired, he looked forlorn. When we closed up I went home to more gloom and uncertainty. The TV was off, I suspect my Mother had once again had her fill. I changed clothes and walked over to Margaret Mary's. She was on the front porch reading.

"Sean is still sleeping," she whispered as I came in. She rose to hug me, limp in my arms, and motioned me to sit next to her on the sofa.

"I keep thinking this is some horrible bad dream and that I'm going to wake up and everything is going to be alright." She said, almost hopefully.

"Everybody is so upset," I replied, "Lefty even closed early. Teddy said nobody's coming into the garage either."

"Did anything else happen today?' She asked, "About the President I mean."

"They charged that Oswald guy with killing him but they didn't say anything else. Lots of people are waiting to see President Kennedy's body."

"Where is it? How are people getting to see it?" She sounded worried, anxious. "Where are Jackie and her children?"

I told her what I knew, about the lying in state, about the long lines of mourners standing in the rain, the funeral planned for Monday and how President Johnson had declared Monday to be a National Day of Mourning.

Margaret Mary sighed and fell back against the sofa and as she did Sean, looking very haggard, emerged from in the house. Margaret Mary would not look at him as he sank into a chair.

"Apologies and deep shame once again my children." Sean began, "I fear I have once again succumbed to the whiskey in my weakness."

Margaret Mary continued to look away. I didn't know what to say. Sean pulled himself from the chair and knelt in front of Margaret Mary.

"I am naught without you dear daughter and too often naught always. Please forgive me."

Margaret Mary relented, as she always would, and leaned forward to hug her father. I felt awkward and rose to go.

"Please stay," Margaret Mark said, "I really need to talk about all this or I'll only start crying again."

I sat back down and Sean did the same.

"Does anybody know why this has happened?" Margaret Mary asked in a low, quavering voice.

"The newspaper says that Oswald guy did it by himself. He said he didn't shoot anybody, that they got the wrong guy." I said.

"He has been charged then?" Sean asked.

"Yeah, the police say he did it, but nothin' about why." I answered.

"Why is the question for another day," Sean offered, "Today it is only that it is and what the world will be like now that this good man is gone."

"It feels like everything is bad and nothing is good and it's always going to be that way." Margaret Mary replied.

"This will pass daughter, as all terrible things do, eventually. When I grieve over your Mother I do not expect to get over it, only through it, for one more day, and as the days pass the grief becomes more familiar, always there, but less burdensome."

"But it never goes away?" She asked shakily.

"Never is a long time, I can only say my grief for your mother remains in my heart and is only lessened by my love for you and for what I hope lies in our future."

I was wise enough to recognize a good time for listening and knew this was the time for me to excuse myself. Father and daughter here were talking about much more than the death of our President.

"I see you have been reading your Dickinson, my daughter. Do you know what Miss Emily herself said about death?"

Margaret Mary's eyes filled with tears as she shook her head slowly from side to side.

He said, "*Unable are the loved to die, for love is immortality.*"

On my way home I wondered how to recover the love to smother my hurt and confusion. I wondered if immortality offered solace. I thought of my family, Margaret Mary, Teddy and the others who inhabited my world and hoped they could heal me from this confusion and decided to trust that somehow they would, that we would find this grief less burdensome. Someday.

The evening's Lowell Sun newspaper trumpeted:

SLAIN PRESIDENT LIES IN STATE

And beneath that:

Mrs. Kennedy Must Tell Children

The subsequent stories remained unread, for now. I had all the details I could endure already.

SUNDAY, NOVEMBER 24, 1963

The next morning we went to Mass early, the 9AM service. The church was full, the sermon a eulogy for our President and an assurance that we would all grieve this man together. Usually in church my mind wandered, today I listened, I needed to be part of as much community as I could muster. The grief I felt was lessened when I grieved with others.

When we returned home the Sunday Morning Lowell Sun headlined:

PIN J.F.K. SLAYING ON OSWALD

And sub-headlined:

"Police Claim They Have Air Tight' Case"

Before I could read any of this Teddy appeared at our front door. My Mother ushered him in. He was carrying his gym bag.

"I'm gonna' go down to the gym, I need to hit somethin'. You wanna' come?" He asked.

I looked to my Mom and Dad. They nodded. My Dad said he'd drive us. As I gathered my things a thought occurred to me.

"Hey Teddy, we should go check on Margaret Mary first. Make sure she's alright."

"Tell them to come over when they want," my Mom added as Teddy and I went out the door.

When we got to Margaret Mary's house she greeted us at the front door. Her eyes were red and swollen with tears. She had on the same clothes she was wearing yesterday. She looked like she hadn't slept all night. I held her tight when we entered and she shook in my arms. Heartache radiated off her like heat.

"Can you help me with Sean, please?" She asked. "I couldn't move him last night."

When Teddy and I moved into the living room Sean was passed out on the floor. The smell of whiskey was strong. He looked more dead than asleep but his body rose and fell with ragged breathing.

"Can we get him into bed please? He's been like that all night."

Teddy and I each took an arm and tried to raise him. He woke, partly, and struggled to his feet. Leaning heavily on Teddy and I we took him down the hall and into his bedroom. He collapsed across the bed and passed out again. Margaret Mary watched sorrowfully from the door.

We went back through the living room and took seats on the front porch. I sat as close as I could to Margaret Mary and put my arm around her.

"I think he'll be okay for a while. You should just let him sleep." I offered. Teddy nodded in agreement as Margaret Mary whispered, "He's never been that bad before. He fell out of the chair and I couldn't wake him up. It's the whiskey you know."

"My Dad was real sad too," Teddy offered. "We went to church last night and everything."

"I just can't understand why anyone would do such a thing." Margaret Mary said, not referring to her father, as that hint of sadness whispered very strong in her voice, "Poor Jacqueline and her children, we lost our president they lost their father."

"The funeral is going to be tomorrow," I added, "We can watch it at my house if you want."

"That would be nice, depending on how my father is feeling." At this point after a brief struggle, she yawned and the fatigue descended on her like a hill of stones.

"Did you sleep at all last night?" I asked.

"A little." She replied wearily, sinking her head farther onto my shoulder. "You should lay down. Me and Teddy will stay here if you want, in case your father wakes up."

Teddy nodded in agreement after I had volunteered him.

"No, we'll be fine. I do need some rest and I'll lay down for a while. What are you two going to do?"

"We were going to go to the gym, bounce around a little." I answered. Anything to get our minds off the ongoing nightmare around us. Boyos and their sporting indeed.

"But we can come over after, to make sure everything's okay if you want." Teddy added.

"That would be very nice." Margret Mary answered, stifling another yawn. We rose to leave and I kissed Margaret Mary goodbye on the cheek as I had been taught grieving people should. Teddy gave her a hug as well. She looked very small and sad and tired as we walked away.

My Dad gave us a ride to the gym and as we got to the parking lot said, "I'm going over to Kay and Dick's to see how they are. I'll swing by on the way home and pick you up."

My Aunt Kay was my Dad's older sister and she never referred to President Kennedy without a huge smile and the expression. "My

President Kennedy". After his election in 1960 I recall my Aunt Kay wearing her "Win With Kennedy" campaign skimmer hat for weeks, with her huge smile. I was glad I didn't have to go see her on this day.

When me and Teddy walked into the gym the mood was subdued, at best. I didn't see Antoine or the Prince but Screwloose was there punishing a speed bag. He waved, I think, when we came in but the other few fighters in the room continued to go about their business without, it seemed, much enthusiasm. Maybe they too just needed to punch something.

"Hi'ya boys", Max called from his office. "Terrible thing, terrible thing", he muttered as he came over to us. "You guys gonna work out?" We nodded.

"When you get changed, I want to introduce you to some new fighters. Terrible thing, terrible thing, ain't it?" Max wandered back into his office.

Just then Butchie, now Kevin, entered the gym. He saw us and came over.

"How are you guy's doin?" He asked, dropping his gym bag on the floor.

We said okay even though we weren't and after a moment Butchie, now Kevin, asked, "Dave can I talk to you alone for a minute?"

Teddy moved off and when we were alone Butchie, now Kevin, asked, "When you were going out with Donna was she, you know, kinda...?" He was really struggling for the word.

"Enthusiastic?" I guessed tactfully.

"Yeah, enthusiastic. Was she?"

"A little," I lied. Why?"

"I'm like worried you know? She might get pregnant or somethin'?"

I knew all about "or somethin'" but I wasn't really comfortable, or experienced enough to talk about such matters. Butchie, now Kevin, was uncomfortable as well. We both shuffled our feet and tried to act casual when the gym door crashed open.

"That Oswald guy just got shot!" Paco Barnes shouted as he rocketed into the gym. Everyone turned to look at him as he repeated, "I heard it on the radio on my way over. He got shot in the police station in Dallas."

More bewilderment, surprise, disbelief that the discord in Dallas could still be going on. What was happening? Why was it happening? When would it stop?

Max turned up the battered radio behind his desk. We bunched in the doorway as the frantic announcer at WLLH reported that a man named Jack Ruby had emerged from a crowd of reporters in the basement of the Dallas Police Station as Oswald was being moved to the city jail. He fired one shot, at point blank range into Oswald's belly. Ruby was wrestled to the ground. Oswald was sped away to the hospital, Parkland Hospital, where President Kennedy had died the day before yesterday.

The crowd in Max's doorway eventually broke up as the announcer reported that basically no one knew what was going on. As we wandered off into the gym I heard Screwloose mutter, "An' peoples think I'm crazy." There seemed to be plenty of crazy to go around.

Butchie, now Kevin, took me aside and said, "Can we keep what we talked about between you and me, about Donna I mean?"

"You bet", I answered, "But be careful Kev, I hope you guys don't get into any trouble or nuthin'".

"Geez, it's killing my roadwork too." Butchie, now Kevin muttered as he headed for the locker room.

Meanwhile President Kennedy's body was being moved to the Rotunda of the Capitol Building as thousands of mourners lined the sidewalks and cued up to view the President's casket. John Fitzgerald Kennedy had been shot twice, once in the head and once in the neck. Closed casket.

Teddy and I changed and wrapped up but I didn't feel much like punching anything anymore. I wanted to sit somewhere and take a lot of deep breaths. I was frightened, uncertain, worried at what was happening in our world. The President, our President, was dead, killed in broad daylight with his wife sitting right next to him, and now the guy who was supposed to have done it was shot too. All in two days, two long, stunning, bewildering days. I thought about how I would tell Margaret Mary when she woke up, if she would be as frightened and confused as I was. I hoped she would not be and knew she would be.

"Hey Teddy," I said, "I'm just gonna' skip some rope."

"I'll be on the bag," he replied, heading for the heavy bags dangling from chains in the far corner of the gym. I was glad to be alone but didn't know why. I started skipping rope trying to get my mind to go anywhere but where it was, stuck thinking about a rainy afternoon in Washington and a closed casket that held the President of the United States.

After a few minutes of skipping rope Butchie, now Kevin came over. Feeling self-conscious I stopped. He asked,

"Whadd'ya think about all this killing that's going on?"

I sagged onto a bench. Butchie, now Kevin sat next to me. We watched the fighters in the gym working out while I gathered my thoughts.

"Everything feels upside down, you know?" I finally answered. "I just can't figure why anybody would want to kill President Kennedy. He was a good guy, wasn't he?"

"My Pop said there were signs up in Dallas saying he was a traitor and he was letting the Communists push us around." Butchie, now Kevin answered.

"But he made the Russians take the missiles out of Cuba and everything." I answered.

"I know, I don't get it either. My Pop said lots of people in the military were really mad at him because the Bay of Pigs invasion failed."

"That wasn't his fault!"

"I'm not sayin' it was, but some people think it was."

That was the hard part, trying to imagine that "some people" didn't love and respect John Kennedy as much as we did. Lowell was certainly not a place where you were likely to hear any criticism of "our president" and he, and his family, were like movie stars, heroes, ideals. And somebody, for some reason, shot him in the head.

"Do you think that Oswald guy did it?" I asked.

"Dunno, the cops say he did, I guess we'll find out soon enough."

We sat and watched the activity in the gym for a while, neither of us able to muster the gumption to get up and hit something, anything. Teddy wasn't having any such problem over on the heavy bag, he was rattling the chains, thumping hard and often on the bag.

"You should go hold that bag for Teddy," Butchie, now Kevin said, "He can hurt his wrists poundin' like that."

So I got up and shouldered into the bag while Teddy banged away. After a few minutes I took a turn, Teddy holding for me and I fell into a rhythm, good, solid smacks that ran all the way up my arm into my shoulders. I broke a sweat, it felt good, my head cleared, I switched off with Teddy and for just that few minutes' life seemed normal again.

"That Oswald guy just died," Max announced from his office door. "Inna room right next to where Kennedy died."

And I lost my wind, my arms and legs felt heavy again, I stopped punching, the uncertainty returned. It was time to go home.

Teddy and I dressed and waited outside for my Dad. Neither of us spoke much, there was nothing to say. When my Dad pulled in I asked him if he heard Oswald was dead.

"Yeah," he replied, "Heard it on the radio on the way over here."

"Now we'll never know why he killed President Kennedy." I replied.

"Worse than that son, now we'll never know if he killed President Kennedy".

"But the police said he did!" Teddy exclaimed from the back seat.

"Yes, they did. But we don't know if anyone helped him. We don't know if he acted alone. We don't know a lot."

These thoughts, echoing those of Butchie, now Kevin, of Peter Rayburn without his beret but seething with anger never occurred to me. Not knowing why it happened was one thing, painful in itself, but not knowing who did it, made matters which seemed like they just couldn't get worse, worse.

The rest of the ride home was silent. Teddy went home and I sat in the living room watching a long line of people file into the Rotunda of the Capitol building to view President Kennedy's body. That's all there was on television, every channel, no commercials, very depressing. I wondered if Margaret Mary was awake yet and decided not to go over just yet in case I would wake her up. I sat and watched TV as long as I could stand it, then decided I would go for a walk, a long walk, just anywhere where the atmosphere might be less gloomy.

Clark Road runs behind the football stadium through a wooded area with few houses on the southern end. Young oaks, birches and elm trees lined both sides. For some ungodly reason people used to discard old furniture and appliances along the more isolated stretches and the moldering and rusty hulks of sofas and washing machines squatted in the roadside woods. Yet mostly it was as close to rustic as

I could get on foot from my house and I went there often to think and wander. Today I was more interested in wandering than thinking.

I could find nowhere to put the events of the past three days in my experience. I had been taught, shown, promised that the good guys would always win. The post-World War II euphoria, Hitler in ashes, Japan humbled, order restored to the world all reinforced the "goodness will triumph" messages all around me. Yet our President, John Fitzgerald Kennedy would see the face of Shannon no more. Jackie was a widow, John Jr. and Caroline fatherless, goodness was in shambles.

I kicked at piles of leaves and threw sticks at obliging trees. I tried to summon my old friends Huck Finn and that Connecticut Yankee who had so confounded King Arthur's Court, they would not come. Matt Dillon, Palladin, even Davy Crocket hung their heads in shame at the crime that had been committed in Dallas and now even an explanation for these shameful events seemed doubtful. My wandering took me past Pow Wow Oak where our Pilgrim forefathers made flimsy treaties with the Wamesit Indians so many years ago. Houses began to dot the road and my footsteps carried me to Hovey Street and then back to Glenmere and to Margaret Mary's door, where a light on the porch told me life had returned.

"Come in, you look so sad," she said after I knocked lightly. But I was more than sad, I was without hope, confounded by the ongoing brutality and without the words to express how I felt. I sat on the sofa, Margaret Mary sat next to me and when she leaned against me I started to cry, all at once and with no control of my tears. Something was gone inside me and I wanted it back. Everything inside me hurt and it would not stop hurting. Margaret Mary put her arms around me as I shook.

"Me too," she whispered as I tried to pull myself together.

"I'm sorry," I croaked when I was out of tears. My cheeks flamed red with embarrassment.

"You have nothing to be sorry for," she replied. "I have been crying all day and I know just how you feel. Everything that is happening is worth crying about."

Several deep breaths later I calmed down. I felt better, not good, just better. We sat in silence for a moment, several moments, until I asked,

"Will you dance with me?"

Margaret Mary looked at me and smiled. Without a word she crossed the room and clicked on her record player. She shuffled through several records and placed one on the turntable. The music began and we danced slowly, in a circle, to the same song, three times. The words rang in my head for the rest of that long sorrowful night:

> *Moon River, wider than a mile,*
> *I'm crossing you in style one day,*
> *Oh dream maker, you heart breaker,*
> *Wherever you're goin', I'm goin' your way.*
> *Two drifters off to see the world*
> *There's such a lot of world to see,*
> *We're after the same rainbow's end,*
> *Waitin' round the bend, my huckleberry friend Moon*
> *River and me.*[10]

I needed to hear and feel something that didn't sound like death and sorrow and sadness. I was never so grateful as right then that Margaret Mary had taught me to dance.

MONDAY, NOVEMBER 25, 1963

The morning arrived all in a hush, with a solemn apprehension permeating the air as the world waited for the state funeral of John Fitzgerald Kennedy to begin. In our home it was exactly as if a member of our own family had died and the services we awaited a personal matter.

---

[10] Johnny Mercer, Henry Mancini, "Moon River".

I rose early that day, without joy, and joined my family over a silent breakfast. There was no school for us this day. All schools, all across the country were closed. All government offices, state and federal were closed. Retail stores did not open, the movie theatres would not open, the libraries were closed, only a very few gas stations were doing business. Lefty's would be closed all day.

The funeral was scheduled to begin at 10:30 in the morning when President Kennedy's body would be taken from the Capitol Rotunda to St. Matthew's Cathedral for a funeral mass conducted by the Archbishop of Boston, Richard Cardinal Cushing.

The long line of mourners waiting to view President Kennedy's body was broken at 8:30. At 9:30 we watched Jacqueline Kennedy, along with Bobby and Ted Kennedy arrive at the Rotunda for a private farewell.

The TV shows us the preparations for the movement of President Kennedy's body. The horse drawn black caisson arrives, the same one which transported Abraham Lincoln's body at his funeral and carried the President from the White House's East Room yesterday. It waits at the bottom of the Rotunda stairs with Black Jack alongside, the saddled but riderless black horse, boots reversed in the stirrups, which will follow the caisson.

The military units who will accompany their Commander in Chief's body form up. The Marine Corps band will lead the procession along with ten pipers from the Scottish Black Watch and 30 Cadets from the Irish Defense Force from Corrah Camp, County Kildare, who were requested by Jacqueline Kennedy to honor her husband's Irish heritage.

Hushed commentary whispers into our living room as we sit transfixed, as if in church ourselves, to witness and to venerate the ceremony. There was a knock on our door as Margaret Mary and Sean arrived. Sean looked dreadful, he was haggard, disheveled in a way I had never seen him before, lifeless, overwhelmed with grief and whiskey. Margaret Mary hugged me, and my Mother, before guiding Sean to a chair like a small child. He sat silent, after nodding a pitiful greeting and watched in silence.

At approximately 10:50 Jacqueline Kennedy along with the President's two brothers emerged from the Rotunda and the procession to St. Matthew's Cathedral began. A million people, they say, lined the streets as the solemn procession passed, led by Jacqueline with Bobby and Ted Kennedy at her side. Her two children followed them in a limousine. Behind the children's car President Lyndon Johnson, accompanied by his wife and two daughters walked the route followed by over two hundred dignitaries from ninety two countries who had arrived for the funeral. President Charles de Gaulle of France was there, along with the British Prime Minister Sir Alec Douglas Hume, The Duke of Edinburgh, President Eamon de Valera of Ireland, representatives from the Soviet Union, Canada, Mexico and many others walked unheralded in the procession.

Amidst the dead silence in our living room was the sound of muffled drums from the military escort along with the plaintive lament of the Black Watch's bagpipes.

Over a thousand invited guests filled St. Matthew's Cathedral for the funeral mass. The service was conducted by the Archbishop of Boston, Richard Cardinal Cushing, a close personal friend of the Kennedy's who had blessed the marriage of John and Jacqueline not so many years before. The television cameras captured it all, the pomp and circumstance along with the reverence, the heartache, the consummate display of deep mourning permeating the services.

In our living room there was silence, a cough, a wiggle, a shifting in a chair, mute observance, and respectful immersion in the proceedings. There was no formal eulogy at the Mass but at the request of Jacqueline Kennedy the Auxiliary Bishop of Washington, Philip Hannah spoke a few words, quoting from the third chapter of Ecclesiastes:

There is an appointed time for everything...a time to be born and a time to die...a time to love and a time to hate...a time of war and a time for peace...

He then read John Kennedy's entire Inaugural address...

"And so my fellow Americans, ask not what your country can do for you, ask what you can do for your country."

A plea cut short, a pledge never to be realized.

Following these remarks a renowned opera singer, Luigi Vena, sang Franz Schubert's "Ave Maria", the hymn he had performed at the wedding of John and Jacqueline Kennedy. During his performance the cameras caught Jacqueline breaking down, sobbing beneath her black veil. Margaret Mary was crying, my Mother was crying, I was strangling on a gigantic lump in my throat, my eyes filled with tears. Sean too sobbed unashamedly into his chest, the only sound he had made all morning. The sadness in our living room was soul deep. And it was going to get worse.

As the President's body was carried from the cathedral at the Mass' end, Jacqueline and her two children stopped at the top of the cathedral's stairs as the casket was placed once again on the caisson. As this was being done, John Kennedy Jr., on what was his third birthday, saluted the departing body of his father. The image, unforgettable on the TV screen, was suspended for all time, in our hearts and minds. My Mother sobbed aloud, Margaret Mary as well. I wiped large tears from my eyes as did my father and a heartbroken, weeping Sean.

President Kennedy's children, we were told, would not accompany their father's body to Arlington Cemetery, across the Potomac. Here on the cathedral steps, after the magnificent salute, they said goodbye to their father. The funeral procession now made its way to Arlington National Cemetery, where only two weeks before President Kennedy had laid a wreath on the Tomb of the Unknown Soldier. A burial site had been prepared at the foot of the slope beneath the Custis-Lee Mansion aligned with both the Lincoln Memorial and the Washington Monument. Jacqueline Kennedy had requested an eternal flame be lit at the gravesite and the U.S. Army Corps of Engineers worked tirelessly through the night to comply with her wish in time for the internment.

At graveside the Corps of Irish Cadets performed a silent ritual, "Queen Anne's Drill" at Jacqueline's request. An Honor Guard folded the flag covering the President's casket and presented it to the widow. Taps was played, the bugler stumbling with emotion on the sixth, heartbreaking note.

At 3:15 Jacqueline Kennedy lit the eternal flame and minutes later President Kennedy's body was lowered into the ground.
In our living room no one moved. We had been sitting for over five hours transfixed by the ceremony, drained of all emotion save sadness. As the television commentary droned on my Mother offered to make sandwiches and she, along with Margaret Mary took to the kitchen. I sat with my Father and brothers, Sean a ghost of a witness, staring at, but not seeing the TV coverage anymore.

"A fine, fine man was buried today," my Father said to his sons. "You should remember this, make a note of his passing, we may never see the likes of him again."

Which was a long speech for my father and one I would never forget. Sean made a sound, a gurgle, and rose from his chair.

"Would you be excusing me," he asked, "I must return to my home. Daughter", he called into the kitchen as Margaret Mary reappeared, "I will take my leave now. Please take your time here. We shall speak when you come home."

He then thanked all of us and left. Margaret Mary stood in the kitchen doorway unsure of whether to follow. My Mother stood beside her and suggested, "Give him a bit of time dear. If he is going to drink again you cannot stop him. If he just needs to be alone so be it. Eat with us, you can go home after."

And so a silent, sad meal was taken, the TV turned off, the images of the day fading ever so slightly into the past. I knew then, right then, that my world was changed forever. A good thing, a fine thing, that Good Man, had been taken away along with all the promise and hope he had spoken of so eloquently during his presidency. With John Kennedy's death my sense of the safety of righteousness had diminished forever. The optimism and potential of a better world, one in which he had once promised to: *"bear any burden, meet any hardship, support any friend, oppose any foe, in order to assure the survival and success of liberty..."* had been shattered, I feared beyond repair. Cynicism and distrust of our government was emerging, becoming part of my behavioral repertoire along with a secret sense of despair.

After a time Margaret Mary said she was going home. I offered to go with her, she asked to go alone. A communion between father and daughter had also been shattered and only they could fix it. We parted on my front stairs and I stood and watched her walk all the way to her home.

As the countless eulogies for John Fitzgerald Kennedy appeared journalists Erwin Glikes and Paul Schwaber wrote...

As those unforgettable days of late November, 1963, drew relentlessly on, it became clear that we had all witnessed one of the dark, random gestures by which chaos reasserts itself in the universe, tearing through the bright patterns we weave about ourselves and call our civilization. Youth, beauty, noble aspirations were struck down before our eyes. It was most properly, a matter of art, for art has met with it before – and will again.

Thus the poet W.H. Auden wrote...

> *Why then? Why there?*
> *Why thus? We cry,*
> *Did he die?*
> *The heavens are silent.*
> *What he was, he was,*
> *What he is fated to become,*
> *How we choose to live,*
> *Will decide its meaning.*
> *When a just man dies*
> *Lamentation and praise*
> *Joy and sorrow*
> *Are One.*

Tales like these, of times like these, most especially those which speak of the death of John Fitzgerald Kennedy, often end with the homily, "Johnny We Hardly Knew Thee."

Known or not, Hardly of Fully, much more than a man died that Friday afternoon on the streets of Dallas, Texas. An ideal, a promise, a personification of what we held as decent and inspiring had died as well. Camelot was in ashes, Jackie in widow's weeds, her children in orphan's attire, the country, it seemed, descending into a kind of darkness we could not yet fully comprehend.

Margaret Mary, Teddy and I would move eventually forward from these days, continue to face new challenges and to struggle with our strengths and weaknesses, but never again with the innocence or the optimism that we had before that fateful day in November of 1963. "Change is the law of life." John Kennedy said, "And those who look only to the past or the present are certain to miss the future."

And so we march ONWARD.

JFK Eternal Flame, Arlington National Cemetery

Davy Crockett

Born on a Mountaintop in Tennessee
Greenest State in the Land of the Free
Raised in the woods so he knew every tree
Kil't him a bear when he was only three...[11]

Somehow.

And that is how we got through it all.

If you enjoyed this book, please take a few moments to write a review on your favorite store, and refer it to your friends. Share your views, how else will anyone know?

---

[11] George Bruns & Thomas Blackburn, The Ballad of Davy Crockett.

CPSIA information can be obtained
at www.ICGtesting.com
Printed in the USA
FSHW022127241120
76118FS